Common Core Writing Handbook

Teacher's Guide

GRADE
2

HOUGHTON MIFFLIN HARCOURT

Contents

Writing Strategies

How to Use This Book

The *Common Core Writing Handbook* was designed to complement the writing instruction in your reading program as well as meet all of the Common Core State Standards for writing. It consists of two components: a handbook for students that they can refer to as a resource as well as practice writing in throughout the year, and a Teacher's Guide that supports instruction by providing minilessons for every handbook topic.

Components

Two easy-to-use components make up the *Common Core Writing Handbook* program:

- For Grades 2–6, a 160-page partially consumable student handbook with 30 writing topics that correlate to your reading program's key writing lessons.

  The first section of each grade-level handbook includes writing models along with interactive practice to scaffold or reinforce students' understanding of opinion, informational/explanatory, and narrative writing. As students practice writing, they build additional examples of forms to refer to throughout the year as well as develop a deeper understanding of each form's structure.

  The second section of the handbook is a resource tool that students can refer to whenever they write. Topics range from writing strategies to how to use technology to do research.

- For Grade 1, a 96-page partially consumable student handbook also includes 30 correlated handbook topics followed by a resource section on writing strategies, such as the writing process and writing traits.

- For Grades K–6, a Teacher's Guide with 60 minilessons for section 1 (two minilessons for each section 1 student handbook topic) plus one minilesson, as needed, for each remaining page of the resource handbook. The Kindergarten Teacher's Guide includes an abundance of copying masters.

Minilessons

Minilessons are short, focused lessons on specific topics. For each minilesson, you will demonstrate an aspect of writing before students try their own hand. In this Teacher's Guide, minilessons are provided for each topic in the handbook. In the first section are two minilessons for each topic. Each of these minilessons consists of the following parts:

- Topic title
- Tab with section name
- Minilesson number and title
- Common Core State Standards
- Objective and guiding question
- Easy-to-follow instruction in an *I Do*, *We Do*, and *You Do* format
- Modeled, collaborative, and independent writing
- Conference and evaluation information

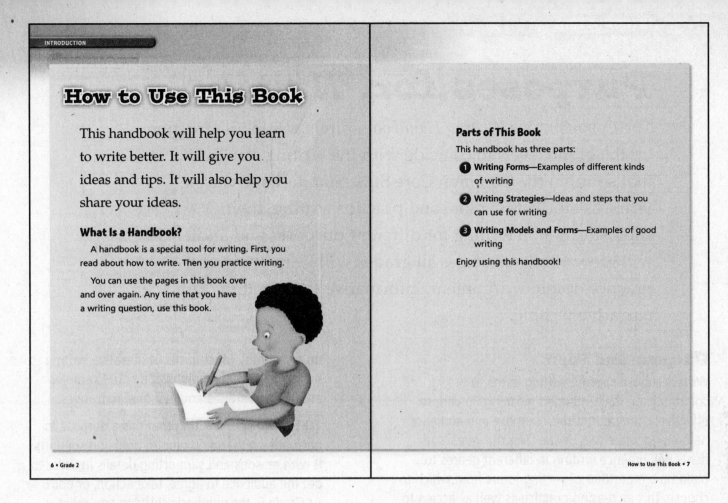

How to Use This Book

This handbook will help you learn to write better. It will give you ideas and tips. It will also help you share your ideas.

What Is a Handbook?

A handbook is a special tool for writing. First, you read about how to write. Then you practice writing.

You can use the pages in this book over and over again. Any time that you have a writing question, use this book.

Parts of This Book

This handbook has three parts:

1 **Writing Forms**—Examples of different kinds of writing

2 **Writing Strategies**—Ideas and steps that you can use for writing

3 **Writing Models and Forms**—Examples of good writing

Enjoy using this handbook!

- Technology references
- Reduced facsimiles of student handbook pages
- Tips for corrective feedback
- A feature that further explores the lesson's writing trait

Each writing minilesson has been correlated to your reading program's writing lessons so that all minilessons and corresponding writing handbook pages within this section are used at least once during the school year. Additional minilessons are provided throughout the Teacher's Guide and correlate to each remaining page in the handbook. Use these minilessons, as needed, to clarify concepts for students and provide additional support.

Student-Page Walk-Through

Have students turn to and read pages 6 and 7 in their books. Explain to them that their handbook is a tool that they can use whenever they write. It can help them find information quickly about any writing question they have, and they can use it to help them during writing. Guide students to find

each of these parts in their handbooks:

- Table of contents
- Introductory pages, including overviews of the writing process and the writing traits
- Writing form pages, each with a section tab, title, definition, and helpful bulleted points, followed by a clear example of the writing model as well as a write-in activity page
- Additional reference pages on topics ranging from writing strategies to revising to using technology, as well as more examples of writing models they may need or want to refer to during the year for projects and other assignments
- An index. Remind students that the table of contents is in order of presentation while the index is ordered alphabetically.

Purposes for Writing

The *Common Core Writing Handbook* spirals writing instruction up the grade levels to coincide with the writing standards that spiral in the Common Core State Standards. Over the years, as students explore and practice writing, their sophistication in writing for different purposes and audiences will grow. Students across all grades will learn about and practice opinion/argument, informative/explanatory, and narrative writing.

Purpose and Form

Writers choose specific writing forms to communicate their intended meaning. To choose effectively, they target their purpose and audience before and while they write. Over the years, students will practice writing in different genres to build up a repertoire of writing forms from which to choose. This increasing practice as well as access to information about writing will help students feel more comfortable about writing and, hopefully, enjoy doing it.

In this handbook, the writing forms and models presented coincide primarily with the purposes expressed through the Common Core State Standards. These are to inform, to explain, to narrate, and to persuade. There are other purposes for writing as well, but these four are emphasized to best prepare students for college and career readiness.

TO INFORM The purpose for writing to inform is to share facts and other information. Informational texts such as reports make statements that are supported by facts and truthful evidence.

TO EXPLAIN The purpose for writing to explain is to tell *what, how,* and *why* about a topic. An example is to explain in writing how to do or make something.

TO NARRATE The purpose of writing to narrate is to tell a story. The story can be made up or truthful. Most forms of narrative writing have a beginning, middle, and end. Examples are fictional stories and personal narratives.

TO PERSUADE Writing that has a purpose to persuade states an opinion or goal and supports it with reasons and supporting details in order to get the audience to agree, take action, or both. At Grade 6, the emphasis shifts to argument.

Over the years, as their writing grows more sophisticated, students may find that their purpose for writing is a hybrid of two or more purposes. An example would be literary nonfiction that includes elements of storytelling although it may be written primarily to inform and explain. Another example would be historical fiction that tells a story but relates events accurately in order to inform the reader as well.

Success in School and Life

Students and adults are often judged by how well they can communicate. Students are encouraged to learn to write effectively to be successful in their studies. In particular, by the upper grades, they need to master the basic essay format that includes

- An introductory paragraph that identifies the topic or statement of purpose.
- Supporting paragraphs that provide related details and examples.

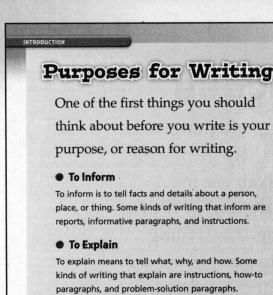

Purposes for Writing

One of the first things you should think about before you write is your purpose, or reason for writing.

● **To Inform**

To inform is to tell facts and details about a person, place, or thing. Some kinds of writing that inform are reports, informative paragraphs, and instructions.

● **To Explain**

To explain means to tell what, why, and how. Some kinds of writing that explain are instructions, how-to paragraphs, and problem-solution paragraphs.

● **To Narrate**

To narrate means to tell a story with a beginning, middle, and end. Some examples of narrative writing include true stories, fiction stories, and biographies.

● **To Persuade**

To persuade means to convince someone else to do something or think a certain way. Some examples are persuasive and opinion essays and book reviews.

Understanding Task, Audience, and Purpose (TAP)

You should also think about your **audience**, or for whom you are writing. For example, the words you use in writing to a friend are likely to be different from those you use with someone you have never met.

You must also choose your **task**, or writing form. For example, if you want to tell your classmates about a topic you have been studying, you can share the information as a report, an essay, or a presentation.

Before you start to write, decide your task, audience, and purpose, or **TAP**. Your task is what you are writing. Your audience is for whom you are writing. Your purpose is why you are writing. Your teacher may give you the TAP for an assignment. Sometimes you will choose on your own.

? Ask yourself these questions.

Task: <u>What</u> am I writing?
  Do I want to write a letter, a report, or something else?

Audience: For <u>whom</u> am I writing?
  Am I writing for a teacher, myself, or someone else?

Purpose: <u>Why</u> am I writing?
  Am I writing to persuade someone, to give information, or for another reason?

● A closing paragraph that sums up and concludes.

Students will use this essay form to produce reports, literary analyses, theses, and critiques throughout their academic career. They will also be tested on their ability to write effective essays in standardized tests. In later life, as adults, they will need to be able to communicate clearly in writing to coworkers, bosses, and clients. This requires extensive and ongoing exposure to exemplary writing models and explicit instruction in a variety of areas, as well as opportunities to practice different forms of writing. In all cases, their purpose for writing must be clear. Evidence suggests that the more time student writers spend on writing, developing their writing skills, and deepening their writing experience, the better writers they become.

The Reading-Writing Connection

The ability to communicate their thinking about texts for a variety of purposes and audiences will serve students well in preparation for college and career readiness. When students write about what they read, reflecting on content, craft, or another aspect of a text, they provide evidence of their thinking. This helps teachers know how well students have understood a text. Additionally, the more students write in response to texts, the more they increase their ability to reflect and improve their critical writing ability. Also, students learn to cite evidence from texts in supporting their claims or supporting their main ideas. This ability becomes particularly useful in writing reports and opinion pieces.

Introduce the Purposes

Have students turn to page 8 and read the text. Explain that these are the key purposes for writing that will be explored in their handbooks. Give or elicit an example of a writing form that might be used for each purpose. Examples might include an informational paragraph or a research report *to inform,* directions or a how-to essay *to explain,* a story or personal narrative *to narrate,* and an opinion essay or letter to the editor *to persuade.* Then have students read the next page. Discuss how students should always consider their TAP—or task, audience, and purpose—to help them better target the message of their writing.

The Writing Process

The *Common Core Writing Handbook* presents the writing process as a strategy that students can use to help them write for any task, audience, or purpose. Students can use the writing process independently or as part of writing workshops in which they respond to each other's writing. The writing process can help students understand how to plan, write, and revise for various purposes and genres. It is thus useful in helping students meet the Common Core State Standards for opinion, informative/explanatory, and narrative writing.

What Process Writing Is

The writing process, or process writing, is an instructional approach to writing that consists of five basic stages. The stages are prewriting, drafting, revising, editing, and publishing. The stages are recursive in nature, meaning that students are encouraged to go back and forth between the stages as needed.

The characteristics of the stages of the writing process are as follows:

Prewriting

This is the stage where students begin to plan their writing. Students:

- Define a task and purpose.
- Identify an audience.
- Brainstorm ideas.
- Narrow and choose a topic.
- Plan and organize information.

Drafting

During drafting, students make their first attempt at fleshing out the prewriting idea and forming it into a written work. In other words, students put their ideas in writing. In this stage, students:

- Write a first draft.
- Do not yet worry about perfecting their writing.

- Know that they can revise, edit, and proofread later.
- Use their plan and checklists to help them write or to return to prewriting, as needed.

Revising

A draft is reread and decisions are made to rework and improve it. In this stage, students might:

- Read aloud their work to others to determine how it sounds and how it might be improved.
- Conference with other students.
- Add information.
- Delete unnecessary information.
- Rearrange sentences and paragraphs.
- Combine sentences.

Editing

During editing, the draft is polished. In this stage, children reread and correct their writing for the following:

- Grammar
- Spelling
- Mechanics
- Usage

The Writing Process

The writing process is a strategy that has five stages. It helps you think of ideas. It also helps you to plan your writing. Finally, it helps you to make your writing better. The best part about the writing process is that you can go back to any of the stages while you're writing.

The writing process helps you move back and forth between the different stages of your writing.

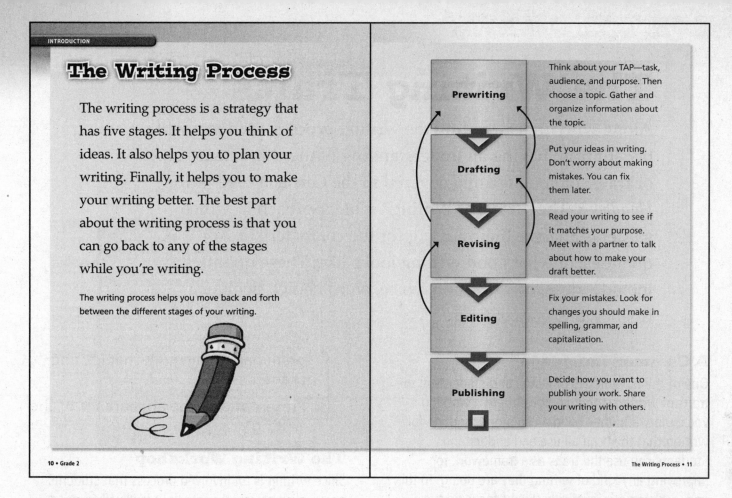

Prewriting — Think about your TAP—task, audience, and purpose. Then choose a topic. Gather and organize information about the topic.

Drafting — Put your ideas in writing. Don't worry about making mistakes. You can fix them later.

Revising — Read your writing to see if it matches your purpose. Meet with a partner to talk about how to make your draft better.

Editing — Fix your mistakes. Look for changes you should make in spelling, grammar, and capitalization.

Publishing — Decide how you want to publish your work. Share your writing with others.

Publishing

Students share their writing with others. In this stage, students typically:

- Make a final, clean copy.
- Use their best handwriting, if writing by hand. If they are sharing their work electronically, they typically choose typefaces and other elements to make their writing readable and attractive.
- Combine their writing with art or graphics.
- Make multiple copies, read their writing aloud, post it electronically, or share and display it in some other way.

Introduce the Process

Have students read pages 10–11. Explain that the writing process is a strategy that they can use to help them write about any topic. Point out how the graphic on page 11 has arrows, indicating that students can go back and forth between the stages as needed. For students who have no previous orientation to the writing process, simplify your introduction by emphasizing at first only the three key stages of planning, drafting, and revising. Elicit how most tasks of any nature require planning, doing or making something, and then thinking about what might be done better and making those improvements. Compare how these same basic stages can be used each time students write.

Have students turn to the table of contents and locate the section in their handbooks devoted to the writing process (pages 74–81). Explain that they can use these handbook pages whenever they need help with specific stages or writing in general. Point out that each stage in the handbook has one or two pages devoted to it that tell more about the stage. As an example, have students turn to the Prewriting pages 76–77, and point out how they show the different organizational plans students can use for the different kinds of writing they will do. Encourage students to use their handbooks as a resource whenever they write.

The Writing Traits

Along with understanding the writing process, students will benefit from having an understanding of the characteristics, or traits, of good writing covered in the *Common Core Writing Handbook.* The "Traits of Writing" is an approach in which students analyze their writing for the characteristics, or qualities, of what good writing looks like. These qualities include ideas, organization, voice, word choice, sentence fluency, and conventions.

A Common Language

One of the advantages of instructing students in the traits of writing is that you give them a working vocabulary and thus build a common language for writing that they can all use and understand. Students can use the traits as a framework for improving any kind of writing they are doing. To this end, a systematic, explicitly taught focus on the traits of writing has proved to be an effective tool for discussing writing, enabling students to analyze and improve their own writing, and providing teachers with a way to assess students' compositions in a fair, even-handed manner.

Writers typically focus on six traits, with presentation—or the appearance of writing— sometimes considered an additional trait.

- **Ideas**—the meaning and development of the message.

- **Organization**—the structure of the writing.

- **Voice**—the tone of the writing, which reveals the writer's personality and affects the audience's interpretation of the message.

- **Word Choice**—the words the writer uses to convey the message.

- **Sentence Fluency**—the flow and rhythm of the writing.

- **Conventions**—the correctness of the grammar, spelling, mechanics, and usage.

- **Presentation**—the appearance of the writing.

The Writing Workshop

Since writing is an involved process that students accomplish at varying speeds, it is usually a good idea to set aside a block of time for them to work on their writing. One time-tested model that has worked well in classrooms is the Writing Workshop. In this model, during a set period of time, students work individually and collaboratively (with classmates and/or with the teacher) on different writing activities. One of these activities is for students to collaborate in reviewing each other's manuscripts. One effective technique used in many workshops as a way for students to comment on aspects of each other's writing is to use the language of the traits when they comment.

Some tasks are started and finished during a workshop, while others are ongoing. A writing workshop can serve many writing-related functions:

- Students can work on a class writing assignment (ongoing or quickly accomplished).

- Students can engage in independent writing, jotting down or consulting ideas in their writing log or journal, starting or working on pieces of their own devising.

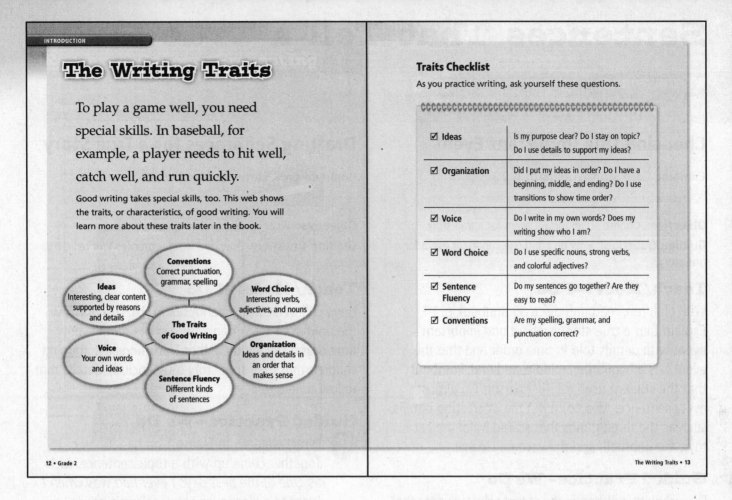

The Writing Traits

To play a game well, you need special skills. In baseball, for example, a player needs to hit well, catch well, and run quickly.

Good writing takes special skills, too. This web shows the traits, or characteristics, of good writing. You will learn more about these traits later in the book.

Conventions
Correct punctuation, grammar, spelling

Ideas
Interesting, clear content supported by reasons and details

Word Choice
Interesting verbs, adjectives, and nouns

The Traits of Good Writing

Voice
Your own words and ideas

Organization
Ideas and details in an order that makes sense

Sentence Fluency
Different kinds of sentences

Traits Checklist
As you practice writing, ask yourself these questions.

☑ Ideas	Is my purpose clear? Do I stay on topic? Do I use details to support my ideas?
☑ Organization	Did I put my ideas in order? Do I have a beginning, middle, and ending? Do I use transitions to show time order?
☑ Voice	Do I write in my own words? Does my writing show who I am?
☑ Word Choice	Do I use specific nouns, strong verbs, and colorful adjectives?
☑ Sentence Fluency	Do my sentences go together? Are they easy to read?
☑ Conventions	Are my spelling, grammar, and punctuation correct?

- As previously mentioned, students can engage in peer-conferencing, giving one another advice about a piece of writing or sharing writing ideas.

- Students can select pieces for inclusion in their writing portfolio, where they keep their best work.

- Teachers can conference with individual students, reviewing student writing and discussing a given student's strengths and weaknesses as well as instructional progress.

- Teachers can engage in small-group instruction with students who need extra help with practice in specific areas of writing.

Writing Workshops are often most effective when they adhere to a dependable schedule and follow a set of clearly posted guidelines (for example, keep voices down, point out the good things about someone's writing as well as comment on aspects that might be revised, listen politely, put away materials when the workshop is over). In addition, students should know what areas of the classroom they can use during the Workshop and should have free access to writing materials, including their handbooks.

You may want to refer to the Writing Workshop pages in this *Common Core Writing Handbook Teacher's Guide* and teach one or two minilessons on writing workshop behaviors and activities so that students have a solid understanding of what is expected of them.

Introduce the Traits

Share the Writing Traits overview pages with students. Discuss each trait briefly and explain to students that their handbooks contain more information on the traits, which they can use to help them as they plan, draft, revise, edit, and publish their writing. Guide students to use their tables of contents or indexes to locate where additional information can be found in their handbooks.

Sentences That Tell a True Story

Minilesson 1

Choosing One Important Event

Common Core State Standard: W.2.3

Objective: Choose an important event for a true story.

Guiding Question: How do I find one important event for a true story?

Teach/Model—I Do

With children, read and discuss handbook p. 14. Explain that a true story is about one important event with details told in time order and that the event has a beginning, middle, and end. Point out that the student used the first person *I* in almost every sentence. Also point out the interesting details, such as the three things that scared Milo: the cat toys, the doorbell, and the vacuum cleaner.

Guided Practice—We Do

Discuss with children some recent school events that were important to them, such as field trips, class activities, and school fundraisers. List the events on the board. Then guide children to choose one event and provide three interesting details about it. As a group, determine whether the event could make a good topic for a true story.

Practice/Apply—You Do

COLLABORATIVE Ask pairs to select two other events from the board and list three interesting details about each. Have children decide which event would make a better story.

INDEPENDENT Have children think of another possible event for a true story. Have them list three interesting details about the topic and decide whether the event would make a good story.

Conference/Evaluate

Circulate, reminding children to ask themselves if the event they chose has enough interesting details.

Minilesson 2

Drafting Sentences for a True Story

Common Core State Standard: W.2.3

Objective: Write sentences that tell a true story.

Guiding Question: How do I write sentences that tell a true story?

Teach/Model—I Do

Have children turn to handbook p. 14. Discuss how the boldfaced transition words in the model show time order. Review the Other Transitions list. Remind children that their true story must include details that follow time order.

Guided Practice—We Do

 Direct children to Frame 1 on handbook p. 15. Together come up with a topic sentence, such as *One of the best days I ever had was when I went to a sleepover at my cousin's house.* Work together with children to complete the frame, using details and noting how transition words help show a beginning, middle, and end. Have children write in their books as you write on the board.

Practice/Apply—You Do

 COLLABORATIVE Ask children to work in pairs to complete Frame 2, using the event they chose in the Collaborative section of Minilesson 1. Remind them to include interesting details as they complete the frame.

 INDEPENDENT Have children read the directions. Tell them to use their prewriting plan from Lesson 1 or to brainstorm new ideas using Graphic Organizer 10.

Conference/Evaluate

During the writing process, circulate and offer encouragement and help as needed. Evaluate using the rubric on p. 104.

Digital
• eBook
• WriteSmart
• Interactive Lessons

Sentences That Tell a True Story

Sentences that tell a true story are always about events that have happened to a writer.

Parts of Sentences That Tell a True Story

- The words *I* and *me*
- Descriptive words that tell how the writer feels
- Events that really happened, told in time order
- Details that help the reader picture the story
- Transition words that show the order of events

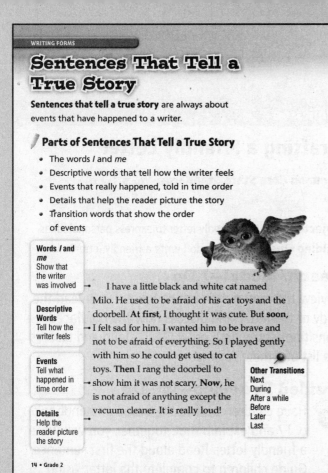

Words *I* and *me*
Show that the writer was involved

Descriptive Words
Tell how the writer feels

Events
Tell what happened in time order

Details
Help the reader picture the story

I have a little black and white cat named Milo. He used to be afraid of his cat toys and the doorbell. **At first,** I thought it was cute. But **soon,** I felt sad for him. I wanted him to be brave and not to be afraid of everything. So I played gently with him so he could get used to cat toys. **Then** I rang the doorbell to show him it was not scary. **Now,** he is not afraid of anything except the vacuum cleaner. It is really loud!

Other Transitions
Next
During
After a while
Before
Later
Last

14 • Grade 2

Name _____

Follow your teacher's directions to complete Frames 1 and 2.

1 One of the best days I ever had was when I _____
_____
In the morning, I _____
_____
_____. Later, _____
_____
At the end of the day, I felt _____

2 _____
_____. In the beginning, _____
_____
_____. After that, _____
_____
_____. Finally, _____

3 On a separate sheet of paper, use your prewriting plan to write sentences that tell a true story about your favorite activity.

Sentences That Tell a True Story • 15

✓ Corrective Feedback

IF . . . children are not including transition words,

THEN . . . remind them to look at the Other Transitions list on page 14 of the handbook. Encourage them to consider the beginning, middle, and end of the event in their writing and to use transition words that reflect those stages of the topic.

Focus Trait: Ideas

Some children might have trouble thinking of ideas. Remind children to freewrite whatever details they remember from their event. Write:

I loved my class trip to the zoo. I went home and told my brother about the trip. Saw monkeys and apes. Rode bus to zoo with friends. Saw baby lions. Waited in long lines.

Then guide children to choose interesting details and put them in time order. Rewrite the example into complete sentences.

I loved my class trip to the zoo. First, I rode the bus to the zoo with my friends. Next, I saw monkeys and apes. I also saw baby lions. Finally, I went home and told my brother about the trip.

Friendly Letter

Minilesson 3

Using Letter Format

Common Core State Standard: L.2.2b

Objective: Write parts of a friendly letter using correct format.

Guiding Question: What are the parts of a friendly letter?

Teach/Model—I Do

Read aloud the definition, parts, and model on handbook p. 16. Point out the five parts of a letter in the model. Explain that *Dear Luke,* is the greeting, *We had so much fun* is part of the body, and *Your friend,* is the closing. Point out the address and date at the top of the letter and the signature at the end. Show children that the greeting and closing always begin with a capital letter and end with a comma.

Guided Practice—We Do

Elicit from children the format for a friendly letter. Together, write the sender's address and date on the board in the correct position. Explain that friendly letters are written to friends or family members. Help children suggest a greeting and a closing for the letter, such as *Dear Aunt Ruth,* and *Love, Your niece.* Demonstrate the correct way to write the greeting and the closing by using capital letters and commas.

Practice/Apply—You Do

COLLABORATIVE Tell groups to practice writing the parts of a friendly letter to the teacher. Have children write the address and date, a greeting, a closing, and the signature. Encourage them to position the parts of the letter correctly.

INDEPENDENT Instruct children to write the parts of a friendly letter to a friend. Tell them to leave space for the body of the letter.

Conference/Evaluate

Circulate and help children with the parts of their friendly letters. Remind them to use capital letters and commas in the greeting and closing.

Minilesson 4

Drafting a Friendly Letter

Common Core State Standards: W.2.3, L.2.2b

Objective: Write a friendly letter to express personal ideas.

Guiding Question: How do I write a friendly letter?

Teach/Model—I Do

Review the material on handbook p. 16. Reread the body of the letter and discuss how the boldfaced transitions show time order. Read aloud and discuss the list of Other Closings.

Guided Practice—We Do

 Have children turn to the frame on handbook p. 17 and explain that, together, you will write a friendly letter. Read aloud the first sentence. Guide children to complete the letter, using their ideas about a visit to a water park. Remind children that the events in the letter should be written in time order. Have children write in their books as you write on the board.

Practice/Apply—You Do

 COLLABORATIVE Have small groups read the directions and write a new letter for Activity 2. Tell them to write events in time order, include their thoughts and feelings, and draw a picture if they wish. Have groups share their letters.

 INDEPENDENT Have children read the directions. Tell them to use their prewriting plan from Lesson 2 or to brainstorm new ideas, using Graphic Organizer 4.

Conference/Evaluate

During the writing process, circulate and offer encouragement and help as needed. Evaluate using the rubric on p. 104.

Digital
• eBook
• WriteSmart
• Interactive Lessons

Friendly Letter

A **friendly letter** has five parts. You write a friendly
letter to someone you know.

Parts of a Friendly Letter

- A heading, greeting, body, closing, and signature
- A reason for writing
- Interesting details
- Your thoughts and feelings

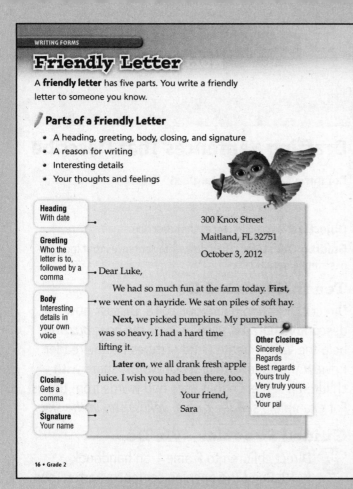

Heading
With date

Greeting
Who the
letter is to,
followed by a
comma

Body
Interesting
details in
your own
voice

Closing
Gets a
comma

Signature
Your name

300 Knox Street

Maitland, FL 32751

October 3, 2012

Dear Luke,

    We had so much fun at the farm today. **First,**
we went on a hayride. We sat on piles of soft hay.

    Next, we picked pumpkins. My pumpkin
was so heavy. I had a hard time
lifting it.

    Later on, we all drank fresh apple
juice. I wish you had been there, too.

        Your friend,

        Sara

Other Closings
Sincerely
Regards
Best regards
Yours truly
Very truly yours
Love
Your pal

Follow your teacher's directions to complete this page.

 1

_____

_____

_____

Dear _____

    We had the best time at the water park. First, _____

_____

_____. Next, _____

_____

_____

_____. Later on, _____

_____

_____

_____

_____

2 On a separate sheet of paper, plan and write a short friendly
letter to your teacher. Include all five parts.

3 On a separate sheet of paper, use your prewriting plan
to write a friendly letter, or make a new plan to write
a letter about a different event. Include all five parts.

✓ Corrective Feedback

IF . . . children are forgetting
to use the correct format for their
friendly letter,

THEN . . . remind them that there are five parts to a friendly
letter, and each part has a specific purpose and style. Explain that
when children write a letter, they must first decide on who the letter
is going to and what the purpose for the letter is going to be.

Focus Trait: Voice

When writing a friendly letter, children should try to
express their own thoughts and feelings. They should
try to write in their own voice as if they are actually
talking to the person. Write on the board:

There were many interesting animals to see.

*The animals made me think about the time you
took me to the zoo and how much fun we had.*

Ask children to read both sentences and think about
which sentence really sounds like a child writing to a
family member.

Then have children reread their own letters. Ask
them to add more words or ideas in their own voice,
reminding them that their words should show how
they really think and feel.

Sentences That Describe

Minilesson 5

Creating a Word Picture

Common Core State Standard: W.2.3

Objective: Write sentences that describe.

Guiding Question: How can I create word pictures for my readers?

Teach/Model—I Do

Read aloud handbook p. 18. Point out descriptive words in the model, such as *green, warm,* and *bright.* Tell children that these kinds of words are called sense words. Explain that sense words help create pictures in a reader's mind. Writers give details about what it is like to see, touch, smell, hear, and taste what they are describing. These details help the reader experience what the writer experienced.

Guided Practice—We Do

Guide children to identify other sense words in the model. Then work together to create more word pictures about the summer season by helping them to complete the following sentences: *I hear_____; I see _____; I taste _____; I smell _____; I touch _____.*

Practice/Apply—You Do

COLLABORATIVE Tell partners to create word pictures about their favorite meal, such as *big, brown meatballs.* Have children write word pictures using the sentence frames from the We Do activity above. Invite children to share their word pictures when they are done.

INDEPENDENT Have children create word pictures about their favorite place. They may use the sentence frames from the We Do activity above and add information to create word pictures. Invite children to share their work when they finish.

Conference/Evaluate

Circulate as children write and help them with their sentences. Remind children that sense words create word pictures.

Minilesson 6

Drafting Sentences That Describe

Common Core State Standard: W.2.3

Objective: Write sentences that describe.

Guiding Question: How do I write sentences that include descriptive details?

Teach/Model—I Do

Direct children to handbook p. 18. Discuss how descriptive phrases, such as *hear the bees buzzing,* help the writer create word pictures for the reader. Review the list of Other Sense Words. Share with children a sentence that uses two words from the list. For example, *I see the round, yellow sun in the sky.*

Guided Practice—We Do

 Direct children to Frame 1 on handbook p. 19. Read the opening sentence starter. Then, ask children to look out the window and share details that they see and hear. Together, come up with a topic sentence, such as *When I look outside the window, I can see tall brown trees.* Ask children, *If you were outside, what would you feel and smell?* Guide them to make suggestions using sense words. Use their responses to complete Frame 1. Have children write in their books as you write on the board.

Practice/Apply—You Do

 COLLABORATIVE Ask children to work in small groups to complete Frame 2 about a common item with which they are familiar, such as a pencil or a piece of chalk. Remind them to include sense words as they complete the frame.

 INDEPENDENT Have children read the directions. Tell them to use their prewriting plan from Lesson 3 or brainstorm new ideas using Graphic Organizer 15.

Conference/Evaluate

During the writing process, circulate and offer encouragement and help as needed. Evaluate using the rubric on p. 104.

Digital
• eBook
• WriteSmart
• Interactive Lessons

Sentences That Describe

Sentences that describe tell the reader all about a person, place, thing, or feeling. They use our senses to show how things look, smell, taste, feel, and sound.

Parts of Sentences That Describe

- One main idea
- Sense words
- Details that are grouped in an order that makes sense

One Main Idea
Describes one thing at a time

Sense Words
Use sights, sounds, tastes, smells, and textures to describe

Details
Are grouped in a way that makes sense

Summer is my very favorite time of year. All of the leaves on the trees are green. The wind blows through them all day. The sun is warm and bright. The grass feels soft on my feet when I take off my shoes. I can smell the flowers and hear the bees buzzing in them. The flowers are pink and yellow and green. They grow near the sidewalk and in front of the porch. But I like summer the best because I can play outside!

Other Sense Words
Round
Blue
Sour
Fast
Loud
Fuzzy
Yellow
Dusty

18 • Grade 2

Name _____

Follow your teacher's directions to complete Frames 1 and 2.

1 When I look outside the window, I can see _____
_____

The air outside feels _____

_____. I can hear the sound of _____
_____

I can smell _____
_____

2 _____

_____. Its shape is _____
_____

_____. It feels _____
_____

_____. When it moves, it sounds _____
_____

3 On a separate sheet of paper, use your prewriting plan to describe your favorite activity, or make a new plan to write about a room you like to be in.

Sentences That Describe • 19

✓ Corrective Feedback

IF . . . children are not including sense words,

THEN . . . remind them to use the sentence frames from the We Do activity from Minilesson 5 on p. 18. Remind children that sense words describe things we see, touch, smell, taste, and hear. Practice with children. For example, *I hear birds chirping. I see green leaves. I feel rough bark.*

Focus Trait: Word Choice

Remind children that the words they use can help paint a picture for their readers. They can replace dull words with more interesting ones that better show their reader what they are describing.

Write the following sentences on the board:

There was a tree.

A bird chirped.

The pie smelled.

Ask children to help you come up with more descriptive sense words for these sentences.

For example:

There was a tree with bright green leaves.

A blue bird chirped like a little flute.

The pie smelled sweet.

Grade 2 • **19**

True Story: Prewriting

Minilesson 7

Purposes for Writing a True Story

Common Core State Standard: W.2.3

Objective: Write a narrative that tells a true story.

Guiding Question: How do I express true ideas in a narrative?

Teach/Model—I Do

Tell children that people write for three reasons: to inform, or give information; to persuade, or give opinions; and to express, or give one's personal thoughts or feelings. Read aloud handbook p. 20. Explain that the model is a plan for a true story, which is one kind of expressive writing. Point out that the details are not the kind you would find in persuasive or informative writing. Point out how each box in the flow chart contains a detail from one true event, *finding Lucky*.

Guided Practice—We Do

On the board, write: *All about my town's history, Why Florida is the best state*, and *The day I moved to town*. Guide children to choose the best topic for a true story. Ask children, does this sound like it will give information, give an opinion, or express details about one true event? Make sure children understand that *The day I moved to town* is the best topic for a true story because it is one true event. Together, list possible details such as *saw my new room, met neighbors, made new friends*.

Practice/Apply—You Do

COLLABORATIVE Ask partners to list three topics. Have children decide if they are good topics for a true story. Finally, have them choose one topic and list related details.

INDEPENDENT Have children list three more topics and decide which would make the best true story. Then have them list three related details.

Conference/Evaluate

Remind children to ask themselves, *Is the purpose of this piece to inform, persuade, or express?*

Minilesson 8

Planning a True Story

Common Core State Standard: W.2.3

Objective: Plan a narrative.

Guiding Question: How do I plan a narrative that is a true story?

Teach/Model—I Do

Have children turn to handbook p. 20. Remind them that brainstorming a topic is the first step in writing a true story, or any kind of narrative. Show children how each topic in the brainstorming list focuses on one event. Point out that the author picked one true event (*How I Found Lucky*) and made a flow chart with details related to the event.

Guided Practice—We Do

 Direct children to Activity 1 on handbook p. 21. With children, brainstorm and list five topics for a true story, writing them on the board as children write in their books. Write *crash from the dining room* as the sixth topic. Tell children to suppose that this is a true event, and have them choose it as the topic for Part B. Guide them to fill out the flow chart with details related to the topic. Have children write in their books as you write on the board.

Practice/Apply—You Do

 COLLABORATIVE Ask partners to list topics for a true story and choose one. Direct each child to fill in a flow chart with events and help each other determine the correct order.

 INDEPENDENT Have children use their prewriting plan from Lesson 4 or brainstorm new ideas using Graphic Organizer 10.

Conference/Evaluate

During the writing process, circulate and offer encouragement and help as needed. Evaluate using the rubric on p. 104.

Digital
• eBook
• WriteSmart
• Interactive Lessons

True Story: Prewriting

A **true story** is always about something real that happened.

Parts of a True Story

- One event that really happened
- A clear beginning, middle, and end
- A starting sentence that tells the main idea
- Important details told in time order

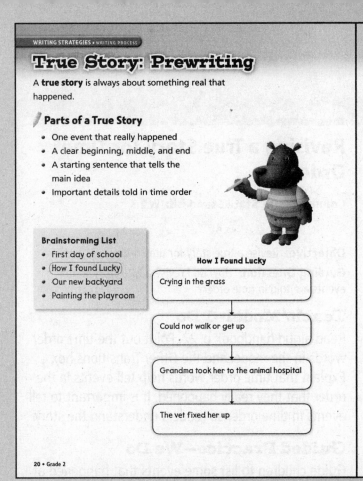

Brainstorming List

- First day of school
- How I found Lucky
- Our new backyard
- Painting the playroom

How I Found Lucky

Crying in the grass

↓

Could not walk or get up

↓

Grandma took her to the animal hospital

↓

The vet fixed her up

Name _____

Follow your teacher's directions to complete this page.

1 a. List of ideas

_____ _____

_____ _____

_____ _____

b. Title or Topic: _____

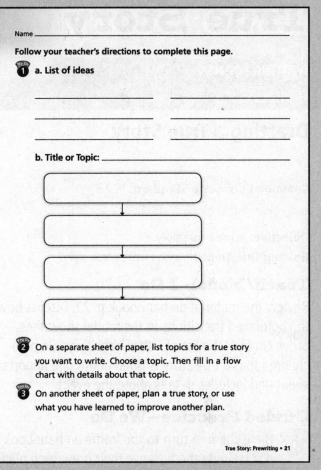

2 On a separate sheet of paper, list topics for a true story you want to write. Choose a topic. Then fill in a flow chart with details about that topic.

3 On another sheet of paper, plan a true story, or use what you have learned to improve another plan.

Corrective Feedback

IF . . . children are having trouble choosing a specific event,

THEN . . . guide children to pick an event with a clear beginning, middle, and end that occurred in one day or less. Show them how to narrow their focus. For example, say, *A true story about summer vacation might be too broad, but a true story about the day you went to the beach is more specific.*

Focus Trait: Ideas

To help children come up with ideas for their true story, have them create a 5Ws chart that lists details about their true event. Practice with children using an example such as the following:

My first day of school

Who?	Me, my parents, my teacher, my best friend, new classmates
What?	Lunch, books, jungle gym
When?	August
Where?	Sunnyside Elementary School, classroom, cafeteria, playground
Why?	Summer ended, first day of 2nd grade

Have children make charts for their own topics, choose details that relate to the topic, and put the details in time order.

# True Story

| Minilesson 9 | Minilesson 10 |

Drafting a True Story

Common Core State Standard: W.2.3

Objective: Write a true story.

Guiding Question: How do I write a true story?

Teach/Model—I Do

Review the material on handbook p. 22. Discuss how the boldfaced transitions in the model show time order. Go over the list of Other Transitions. Remind children that a true story is often about one important event and includes details about the event.

Guided Practice—We Do

 Have children turn to the frame on handbook p. 23. Guide them to use their prewriting plans from Minilesson 8 to write a story, using the time order words as a guide. Have children write in their books as you write on the board.

Practice/Apply—You Do

 COLLABORATIVE Have partners work together to write a new story for Activity 2. Remind them to tell about one important event, give details in time order, and include an ending that wraps up the story. Encourage them to use prewriting as necessary to help them brainstorm ideas.

 INDEPENDENT Have children read the directions. Tell them to use their prewriting plan from Lesson 5 or to brainstorm new ideas, using Graphic Organizer 4.

Conference/Evaluate

During the writing process, circulate and offer encouragement and help as needed. Evaluate using the rubric on p. 104.

Revising a True Story for Time Order

Common Core State Standard: W.2.3

Objective: Revise a true story for time order.

Guiding Question: How do I revise a true story so that events are told in time order?

Teach/Model—I Do

Read aloud handbook p. 22. Point out the time order words in the model and the Other Transitions box. Explain that time order words help tell events in the order that they really happened. It is important to tell events in time order so readers understand the story.

Guided Practice—We Do

Guide children to list some events that happened at school today, such as *sang the school song; went to assembly; said hello to our friends.* Write their ideas on the board. Together, rewrite the events in the order in which they happened. Guide children to add time order words. For example, ***First****, we said hello to our friends.* ***Then****, we went to assembly.* ***During*** *assembly, we sang the school song.*

Practice/Apply—You Do

COLLABORATIVE Direct children to handbook p. 23. Have partners revise the true story they wrote for Activity 2. Have them place events in the order in which they happened and add time order words where needed.

INDEPENDENT Have children revise their true story drafts from Activity 3, making sure events are in order and time order words are used correctly.

Conference/Evaluate

Circulate and help children place time order words in the right places.

 Digital
- eBook
- WriteSmart
- Interactive Lessons

True Story

A **true story** is about something that really happened.

Parts of a True Story

- A beginning, a middle, and an ending
- A beginning sentence that gets readers interested and tells the main idea
- One important event that really happened
- Details told in time order

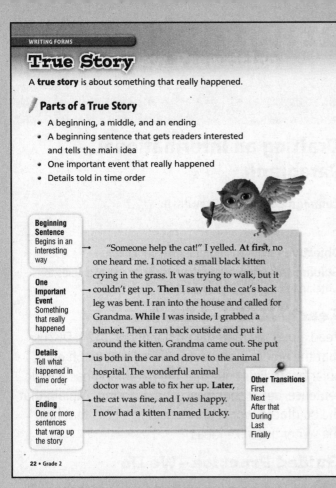

Beginning Sentence
Begins in an interesting way

One Important Event
Something that really happened

Details
Tell what happened in time order

Ending
One or more sentences that wrap up the story

"Someone help the cat!" I yelled. **At first**, no one heard me. I noticed a small black kitten crying in the grass. It was trying to walk, but it couldn't get up. **Then** I saw that the cat's back leg was bent. I ran into the house and called for Grandma. **While** I was inside, I grabbed a blanket. Then I ran back outside and put it around the kitten. Grandma came out. She put us both in the car and drove to the animal hospital. The wonderful animal doctor was able to fix her up. **Later**, the cat was fine, and I was happy. I now had a kitten I named Lucky.

Other Transitions
First
Next
After that
During
Last
Finally

22 • Grade 2

Name _____

Follow your teacher's directions to complete this page.

1 Boom! I heard a loud crash from our dining room.

At first, _____

_____. Then _____

_____. While _____

_____

_____. I was so _____

_____

Later, _____

_____. Next, _____

_____. After that, _____

_____. Finally, _____

_____

_____

2 On a sheet of paper, write a true story about a time you tried something new.

3 On a sheet of paper, use your prewriting plan to write a true story. If you like, make a new plan and write about something that happened to you.

True Story • 23

Corrective Feedback

IF . . . children are having trouble ending their true stories,

THEN . . . remind them that the ending should wrap up the story. It can also tell how the writer felt about the event. Encourage children to use Graphic Organizer 4. In the last box, they can write their feelings. Then they can add those feelings to the ending of their personal narrative.

Focus Trait: Sentence Fluency

Explain to children that combining ideas into longer, smoother sentences can make writing clearer and easier to read. Using different sentence beginnings can also help one event flow to another. On the board, write the following: *My family went on a trip. My family went on a trip to New York City. First, my family saw a musical. Then, my family saw a base-ball game. My family cheered for our favorite team.*

Work with children to combine sentences and use a variety of sentence beginnings. For example, *My family went on a trip to New York City. First, we saw a musical. Then, we saw a baseball game, and my sister and I cheered for our favorite team.*

Informational Paragraph

Minilesson 11

Planning a Main Idea and Details

Common Core State Standards: W.2.2, W.2.8

Objective: Write to inform using facts and examples.

Guiding Question: How do I plan to write about a main idea and details?

Teach/Model—I Do

Read aloud handbook p. 24. Explain that the main idea of the model is *Polar bears live in dens in the far north*. Review the details that tell about the main idea, such as *They dig the dens out of snow and ice*. On the board, organize the information about polar bears into Graphic Organizer 7. Explain that the map can be a plan for an informational paragraph.

Guided Practice—We Do

Help children write a main idea about beaver homes. Example: *Beavers build dams*. Draw Graphic Organizer 7 on the board, and guide children to list details that support the main idea, such as *made of sticks of wood, look like a hill, built in ponds or streams*.

Practice/Apply—You Do

COLLABORATIVE Provide reference sources and have partners fill out an idea-support map for the main idea, *Turtles protect themselves in many ways*. Have children list details, such as *hide their heads in their shells; swim quickly; bite*.

INDEPENDENT Have children fill out an idea-support map about another animal. Remind them to make sure the details support, or tell about, the main idea.

Conference/Evaluate

Circulate, helping children choose details that relate to their main ideas.

Minilesson 12

Drafting an Informational Paragraph

Common Core State Standard: W.2.2

Objective: Write an informational paragraph.

Guiding Question: How can I use facts and examples to write an informational paragraph?

Teach/Model—I Do

Read aloud the material on handbook p. 24. Discuss that the model is an informational paragraph on polar bears. Point out that the paragraph has a topic sentence, detail sentences, and a closing. Explain that the boldfaced words are transition words that help the writer organize ideas.

Guided Practice—We Do

 Have children turn to Frame 1 on handbook p. 25, and explain that they will write an informational paragraph. Guide children to write about a beaver home, using facts gathered in Minilesson 11. Together, complete the topic sentence (about dams) and add facts and details to complete the paragraph.

Practice/Apply—You Do

 COLLABORATIVE Have partners work together to write a new informational paragraph for Frame 2. Have them use their plan from Minilesson 11. Ask children to include a topic sentence and supporting sentences.

 INDEPENDENT Have children read the directions. Tell them to use their prewriting plan from Lesson 6 or to brainstorm new ideas, using Graphic Organizer 7.

Conference/Evaluate

During the writing process, circulate and offer encouragement and help as needed. Evaluate using the rubric on p. 104.

Digital
- eBook
- WriteSmart
- Interactive Lessons

Informational Paragraph

An **informational paragraph** gives facts about one main idea or topic. An informational paragraph also gives details that support the main idea.

Parts of an Informational Paragraph

- A topic sentence that states the main idea
- Supporting details that tell about the main idea
- Facts that can be proved true
- A closing statement that ties ideas together

Topic Sentence
Tells the topic and main idea

Supporting Details
Facts that tell more about the main idea

Polar bears live in dens in the far north. They dig the dens out of snow and ice. Their fur helps them stay warm in their cold, snowy homes. **Sometimes** they dig their homes in the middle of a snow bank. Most polar bears dig their dens in the fall. **Then** they give birth to cubs in the winter. The mother bear stays in the den with the cubs until the spring. She helps keep them safe. A polar bear's den makes a good home.

Other Transitions
First
Next
One thing
Another thing
Another example
Also
At times

Name _____

Follow your teacher's directions to complete Frames 1 and 2.

1 Many animals build nests, but beavers build _____

_____

_____ (detail) _____

_____ (detail) _____

(detail) _____

2 _____

_____ (detail) _____

_____ (detail) _____

_____

_____ (detail) _____

_____

3 On a separate sheet of paper, use your prewriting plan to write an informational paragraph. If you like, make a new plan to write about a different animal home.

Corrective Feedback

IF . . . children have difficulty finding interesting facts for their informational paragraphs,

THEN . . . remind them to ask themselves questions as they write. Once they choose their topic, they should ask themselves questions such as, *What does the home look like? Where is it built? How is it made?* Encourage children to use the model on handbook p. 24 to help them recall what facts are and how to add information to their paragraphs.

Focus Trait: Ideas

Remind children that they can brainstorm ideas for an informational paragraph by using a web. Model the process of choosing a topic. Draw a web (Graphic Organizer 15) on the board. Have children volunteer a broad topic for the center circle, such as *hobbies*. Then guide children to suggest topics related to hobbies, such as *soccer* and *painting*. Have children think of related topics, and add ideas to the web until it shows several possible topics. Show students how a word web helps writers map out a wide variety of ideas and find a specific, interesting topic.

Informational Paragraph

Minilesson 13

Writing Interesting Facts

Common Core State Standard: W.2.2

Objective: Write interesting facts.

Guiding Question: How can I write interesting facts?

Teach/Model—I Do

Read aloud handbook p. 26. Point out the facts in the model, such as *Groundhogs...have strong muscles for digging deep holes.* Explain that a fact is true information and that interesting facts tell about the main idea in a way that makes readers want to learn more.

Guided Practice—We Do

Write the following questions on the board: *What do giraffes look like? What do they eat? Where do they live?* Read the questions aloud and work with children to answer them. Record their answers on the board using full sentences, such as *Giraffes have a long neck, four legs, and a brown and white coat. They eat leaves and twigs. They live in Africa in the grasslands.* Explain that these answers are facts.

Practice/Apply—You Do

COLLABORATIVE Have small groups of children work together to share three interesting facts about turtles; for example: *Turtles are fast swimmers. They have hard shells that protect them from other animals. They lay eggs.*

INDEPENDENT Ask children to write three more interesting facts about turtles. If they have difficulty thinking of three facts, remind them to ask themselves questions, such as *Where do turtles live? What do turtles eat?*

Conference/Evaluate

Circulate and help children come up with facts. Remind children that asking questions will help them think of interesting facts to write about.

Minilesson 14

Drafting an Informational Paragraph

Common Core State Standard: W.2.2

Objective: Write an informational paragraph.

Guiding Question: How do I use facts and details to write an informational paragraph?

Teach/Model—I Do

Have children turn to the model on handbook p. 26. Point out the main idea in the first sentence. Discuss how the boldfaced words in the model give support to the main idea. Explain that words such as *for example* let us know the sentence is going to tell us more details about the groundhog. Review the list of Other Words That Support the Main Idea. Remind children that every sentence in the paragraph is a fact and relates to, or supports, the main topic.

Guided Practice—We Do

 Direct children to Frame 1 on handbook page 27. Work together to complete the frame, using information they listed in Minilesson 13 about turtles. Remind them that supporting words, such as *also* and *for example*, help relate additional facts to the topic. Have children write in their books as you write on the board.

Practice/Apply—You Do

 COLLABORATIVE Ask children to work in small groups to complete Frame 2 using a common talent or activity as the topic. Remind them to consider the meaning of the transition words as they complete the frame.

 INDEPENDENT Have children read the directions for Activity 3. Tell them to use their prewriting plan from Lesson 7 or to brainstorm new ideas using Graphic Organizer 6.

Conference/Evaluate

During the writing process, circulate and offer encouragement and help as needed. Evaluate using the rubric on p. 104.

Digital
• eBook
• WriteSmart
• Interactive Lessons

Informational Paragraph

An **informational paragraph** explains all about a person, a place, a thing, or even an activity.

Parts of an Informational Paragraph

- A topic sentence that starts the paragraph
- Facts and details that explain the main idea
- A closing sentence that ties ideas together

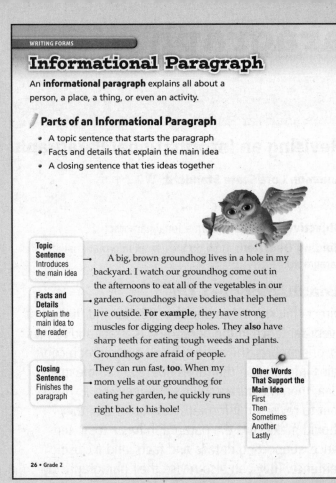

Topic Sentence
Introduces the main idea

Facts and Details
Explain the main idea to the reader

Closing Sentence
Finishes the paragraph

A big, brown groundhog lives in a hole in my backyard. I watch our groundhog come out in the afternoons to eat all of the vegetables in our garden. Groundhogs have bodies that help them live outside. **For example**, they have strong muscles for digging deep holes. They **also** have sharp teeth for eating tough weeds and plants. Groundhogs are afraid of people. They can run fast, **too**. When my mom yells at our groundhog for eating her garden, he quickly runs right back to his hole!

Other Words That Support the Main Idea
First
Then
Sometimes
Another
Lastly

Name _____

Follow your teacher's directions to complete Frames 1 and 2.

1 One animal that I know a lot about is a _____

_____

First, this animal has _____

_____

_____ Also, _____

_____. For example, _____

The best thing about this animal is _____

_____

2 _____

_____ Sometimes _____

_____

_____. In addition, _____

_____. Last, _____

3 On a separate sheet of paper, use your prewriting plan to write about a favorite activity, or make a new plan to write about an invention you would like to make.

✔ Corrective Feedback

IF . . . children are including opinions rather than facts,

THEN . . . remind them that all facts are true and can be proven in some way. Opinions are statements that usually express personal feelings or thoughts and cannot be proven. Have children ask themselves, "Is this how I feel, or is this a statement that is true and could be proven?" Direct children to ask questions about their topic (as in Minilesson 13) to find interesting facts to include.

Focus Trait: Organization

Remind children that informational paragraphs are organized in a way that makes sense. On the board, write the three parts of an informational paragraph:

Introduction: an opening sentence that tells readers about the main idea, or topic

Body: all the facts, connected by supporting words such as also, in addition, *and* for example

Conclusion: the main idea of the paragraph stated in a way that is different from the beginning

Direct children to find the introduction, body, and conclusion in their informational paragraph. Tell children to add whatever is missing from their paragraph's organization, such as a topic sentence or supporting words.

Informational Paragraph

Minilesson 15

Drafting an Informational Paragraph

Common Core State Standard: W.2.2

Objective: Draft an informational paragraph.

Guiding Question: How do I write a draft for an informational paragraph?

Teach/Model—I Do

Read aloud the definition and Parts of an Informational Paragraph on handbook p. 28. Explain that an informational paragraph includes details that relate only to the topic. Read the student model with children, noting the closing sentence that wraps up the paragraph. Finally, direct children to the box of Other Words that Support the Main Idea. Explain to them that these words connect details to the main topic of the paragraph.

Guided Practice—We Do

 Direct children to Frame 1 on handbook p. 29. Guide them to complete the first sentence. For example, *Rainy days can be fun for doing arts and crafts indoors.* Work together with children to complete the frame. Have children write in their books as you write on the board.

Practice/Apply—You Do

 COLLABORATIVE Ask children to work in pairs to complete Frame 2 using an outdoor activity as the topic. Remind them to consider the meaning of the transition words as they complete the frame.

 INDEPENDENT Have children read the directions. Tell them to use their prewriting plan from Lesson 8 or to brainstorm new ideas using Graphic Organizer 15.

Conference/Evaluate

Circulate and help children choose details that relate to the topics they have chosen. Remind them to use a closing sentence to finish their work.

Minilesson 16

Revising an Informational Paragraph

Common Core State Standard: W.2.2

Objective: Revise an informational paragraph.

Guiding Question: How do I revise an informational paragraph?

Teach/Model—I Do

Direct children to handbook p. 28. Remind them that every sentence in the paragraph is a fact and relates to, or supports, the main topic. If a paragraph contains information that does not relate to the main idea, then the paragraph must be revised. Explain that to revise an informational paragraph, they should make sure the paragraph has a topic sentence, supporting details and facts, and a closing sentence. They can also revise their paragraphs by removing details that do not support the main idea.

Guided Practice—We Do

Direct children to Frame 1 on handbook p. 29. Guide children to make sure the paragraph contains each part listed in the Parts of an Informational Paragraph list on p. 28. Help children to remove any details that may not relate to the topic and to add ones that do.

Practice/Apply—You Do

COLLABORATIVE Have partners revise their drafts from Frame 2 on handbook p. 29. Remind them to include topic and closing sentences and remove any unrelated facts.

INDEPENDENT Have children revise their drafts from Activity 3 on handbook p. 29. Tell them to use the rubric on p. 104 to evaluate their work.

Conference/Evaluate

During the writing process, circulate and offer encouragement and help as needed. Evaluate using the rubric on p. 104.

Digital
- eBook
- WriteSmart
- Interactive Lessons

Informational Paragraph

An **informational paragraph** explains something to a reader. It uses facts and definitions to explain and inform.

Parts of an Informational Paragraph

- A topic sentence that tells the main idea
- Supporting details that tell important facts about the main idea
- A closing sentence that finishes the paragraph

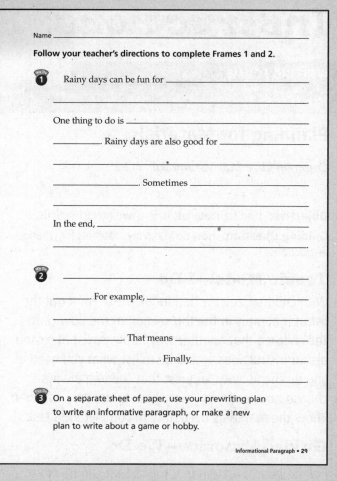

Topic Sentence
Begins the paragraph

Supporting Details
Tell important facts about the main idea

Closing Sentence
Finishes the paragraph

Rain water can be used for lots of things. Every time it rains, my mom puts out a big bucket. When it fills up with water, she puts the bucket on the porch. She uses the water for her plants inside the house. **Also**, she uses the water to rinse my mud projects off the sidewalk. Rain water is good for outside plants, **too**. When it gets hot and sunny, we use the bucket of water for the garden. Mom says we are conserving water. That **means** that we are saving it for a rainy day!

Other Words that Support the Main Idea
In addition
Plus
Next
For example
Last
Then

Name _____

Follow your teacher's directions to complete Frames 1 and 2.

 1 Rainy days can be fun for _____

_____

One thing to do is _____

_____. Rainy days are also good for _____

_____

_____. Sometimes _____

_____

In the end, _____

_____

2 _____

_____. For example, _____

_____

_____. That means _____

_____. Finally, _____

_____

 3 On a separate sheet of paper, use your prewriting plan to write an informative paragraph, or make a new plan to write about a game or hobby.

✔ Corrective Feedback

IF . . . children are struggling to write clear informational paragraphs,

THEN . . . suggest that they include a definition either as the topic sentence or directly following the topic sentence. Explain that informational paragraphs may contain material that is new to readers, so writers often include definitions to make paragraphs easier to understand. For example, a paragraph about mammals might be made clearer by adding the definition, *Mammals are warm-blooded animals with hair on their bodies.*

Focus Trait: Voice

Remind children that a writer's voice should match the purpose of the writing. An informational paragraph should use more formal words to create a formal voice. On the board, write sentences with informal language, such as,

Rainy days can be good for doing stuff indoors.

Baseball is so cool.

Then have children suggest ways to rewrite senten ces with more specific, formal words.

Example:

Rainy days can be good for playing indoors.

Baseball is an exciting hobby.

Instructions: Prewriting

Minilesson 17

Planning for Materials

Common Core State Standard: W.2.2

Objective: Plan for materials before writing instructions.

Guiding Question: How do I plan my materials for writing instructions?

Teach/Model—I Do

With children, review handbook p. 30. Point out the list of materials in the top section of the flow chart. Tell children that another way to plan a list of materials for instructions would be to list what you need as you do the activity. Suggest that children always choose activities they know how to do; they will then know the materials necessary to complete the task.

Guided Practice—We Do

On the board, write a few topics that can be managed in the classroom, such as *How to tie a shoe, how to make a pop-up birthday card,* or *how to draw a turkey* (using your hand as an outline). For *how to tie a shoe,* tell children that only a shoe is needed to do the activity. Guide children to determine whether more materials are needed by having them actually tie their shoes. For example, children might add *laces* or *both hands.*

Practice/Apply—You Do

COLLABORATIVE Have small groups work together to brainstorm some how-to activities, such as how to cover a book, that can be done in class. Ask children to choose one activity, write a list of materials for it, and then try to do the task to determine whether or not more materials are needed.

INDEPENDENT Ask children to choose another task that can be done in class. Have them list the necessary materials and then try the task to determine whether further materials are needed.

Conference/Evaluate

Circulate and help children come up with topics that are safe and appropriate for the classroom.

Minilesson 18

Using Numbered Steps or Sentences

Common Core State Standard: W.2.2

Objective: Use numbered steps in instructions.

Guiding Question: How do I use numbered steps or sentences in instructions?

Teach/Model—I Do

Have children turn to handbook p. 30. Point out the Brainstorming List and the four steps in the student model. Tell children that, if the instructions are not in the proper order, the task will not be done correctly. For example, if the first step were *Spread on two kinds of jelly,* there would be confusion and a messy table.

Guided Practice—We Do

 Direct children to Activity 1 on handbook p. 31. On the board, write the topic *How to Plant Flower Seeds,* followed by the list of materials. Together, list all of the steps for planting flower seeds, such as *1) Fill pot almost to the top with dirt. 2) Make a small hole in center of the dirt. Drop flower seeds in hole. 3) Cover seeds lightly with dirt and water. 4) Place pot in a sunny spot.* With children's help, review all steps and check that they are numbered correctly.

Practice/Apply—You Do

 COLLABORATIVE Have children work in small groups to complete Activity 2 using a task that they are familiar with, such as making cut-out snowflakes. Remind them to include a list of materials and to make sure steps are in order.

INDEPENDENT Have children read the directions. Tell them to use their prewriting plan from Lesson 9 or to brainstorm new ideas using Graphic Organizer 4.

Conference/Evaluate

During the writing process, circulate and offer encouragement and help as needed. Evaluate using the rubric on p. 104.

Digital
- eBook
- WriteSmart
- Interactive Lessons

Instructions: Prewriting

Instructions tell readers how to do something. They include all the steps in order from the beginning to the end.

Parts of Instructions

- A list of materials
- All of the steps in time order
- A clear beginning, middle, and end

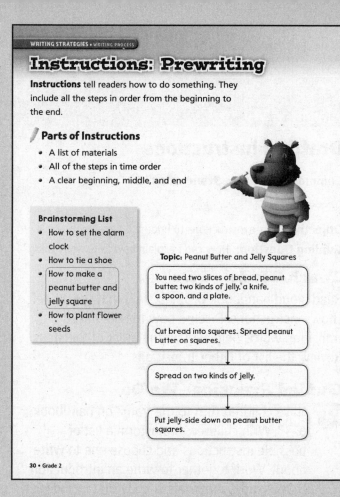

Brainstorming List
- How to set the alarm clock
- How to tie a shoe
- How to make a peanut butter and jelly square
- How to plant flower seeds

Topic: Peanut Butter and Jelly Squares

> You need two slices of bread, peanut butter, two kinds of jelly, a knife, a spoon, and a plate.

↓

> Cut bread into squares. Spread peanut butter on squares.

↓

> Spread on two kinds of jelly.

↓

> Put jelly-side down on peanut butter squares.

Name _____

Follow your teacher's directions to complete this page.

1

How to Plant Flower Seeds

Materials:

Seeds   Flower Pot

Dirt and water   Spoon

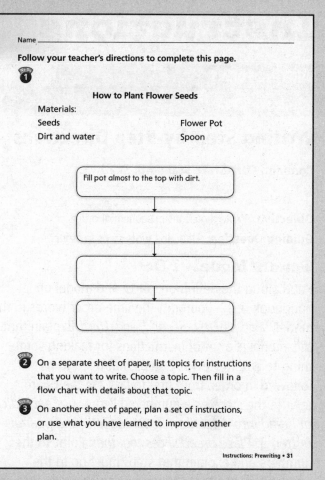

> Fill pot almost to the top with dirt.

↓

>

↓

>

↓

>

2 On a separate sheet of paper, list topics for instructions that you want to write. Choose a topic. Then fill in a flow chart with details about that topic.

3 On another sheet of paper, plan a set of instructions, or use what you have learned to improve another plan.

 ## Corrective Feedback

IF . . . children are missing steps in their instructions,

THEN . . . have them actually do the task based on their own instructions, or act out the task if it cannot be done in the classroom. Tell them to add any missing steps as they complete the task. Suggest that children exchange instructions with a classmate who can help check their steps.

 ## Focus Trait: Ideas

Children may struggle to think of tasks that they can instruct someone else to do. Remind them that they can come up with ideas for their instructions by brainstorming.

To brainstorm activities that they know well, have children make lists about general topics, such as,

Sports That I Play

Hobbies That I Do

Foods That I Make

Arts and Crafts That I Make

Tasks That I Do Every Day

They should write several activities for at least two subjects. Then children should circle the activity they know the best and use this as the topic for their instructions.

Instructions

Minilesson 19

Writing Step-by-Step Directions

Common Core State Standard: W.2.2

Objective: Write directions in sequential order.

Guiding Question: How do I write steps in order?

Teach/Model—I Do

Read aloud the definition, parts, and model on handbook p. 32. Point out the time-order words in the model, such as *First, Second,* and *Third*. Explain that this model is a set of instructions for making something to eat. Review the steps that need to be followed in order, from first to last. On the board, rewrite the steps as a numbered list: *1. Cut each slice of bread into 4 squares, 2. Spread jelly and peanut butter, 3. Place bread slices together.* Point to the numbers and explain that steps must go in the correct order so that the reader can finish the project correctly.

Guided Practice—We Do

Have children think about the steps they would follow for a fire drill. On the board, write *What to Do in a Fire Drill*. Help children brainstorm what they need to do first, such as *Do not talk*, and second, *Follow the teacher's directions*. Write the steps on the board in a numbered list. Explain that these are the first steps to follow during a fire drill.

Practice/Apply—You Do

COLLABORATIVE Tell small groups to work together to write the first two steps for a favorite game in a numbered list. Remind them to first choose the game and write a title for it. Then have children work together to write the first two steps.

INDEPENDENT Ask children to write the first two steps to follow when brushing their teeth, such as *get the toothpaste; squeeze it onto the toothbrush*.

Conference/Evaluate

Circulate and help children with their step-by-step directions. Be sure that they have written the steps in a logical order.

Minilesson 20

Drafting Instructions

Common Core State Standard: W.2.2

Objective: Write instructions to inform.

Guiding Question: How can I explain how to do something?

Teach/Model—I Do

Read aloud handbook p. 32. Explain that the model shows instructions. Discuss how the boldfaced transition words help explain the order of the steps. Review the list of Other Transitions.

Guided Practice—We Do

 Have children turn to the frame on handbook p. 33. With children, brainstorm a list of possible instructions and choose one to write about. Work together to write an introduction that includes materials, a body that includes the steps, and a conclusion that tells what you did. Have children write in their books as you write on the board.

Practice/Apply—You Do

 COLLABORATIVE For Activity 2, have small groups work together to choose a craft project and write instructions. Remind them to list the materials they would need and write the steps in time order. Have groups share their instructions.

 INDEPENDENT Have children read the directions. Tell them to use their prewriting plan from Lesson 10 or to brainstorm new ideas using Graphic Organizer 4. Remind them to add time-order words and a conclusion.

Conference/Evaluate

During the writing process, circulate and offer encouragement and help as needed. Evaluate using the rubric on p. 104.

 Digital
- eBook
- WriteSmart
- Interactive Lessons

Instructions

Instructions tell how to do something. They give steps to follow. Instructions have time-order words to help you write the steps in order.

Parts of Instructions

- Materials your readers need
- Steps to follow in order
- Time-order words
- An ending

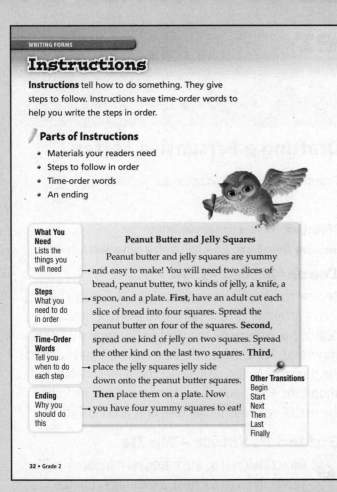

What You Need Lists the things you will need	**Peanut Butter and Jelly Squares**
Steps What you need to do in order	Peanut butter and jelly squares are yummy and easy to make! You will need two slices of bread, peanut butter, two kinds of jelly, a knife, a spoon, and a plate. **First,** have an adult cut each slice of bread into four squares. Spread the peanut butter on four of the squares. **Second,** spread one kind of jelly on two squares. Spread the other kind on the last two squares. **Third,** place the jelly squares jelly side down onto the peanut butter squares. **Then** place them on a plate. Now you have four yummy squares to eat!
Time-Order Words Tell you when to do each step	
Ending Why you should do this	

Other Transitions
Begin
Start
Next
Then
Last
Finally

Name _____

Follow your teacher's directions to complete the frame.

 1 _____

You will need _____
_____
_____

First, _____
_____

_____ Second, _____
_____

Third, _____
_____

_____ Fourth, _____
_____ Last, _____
_____
_____

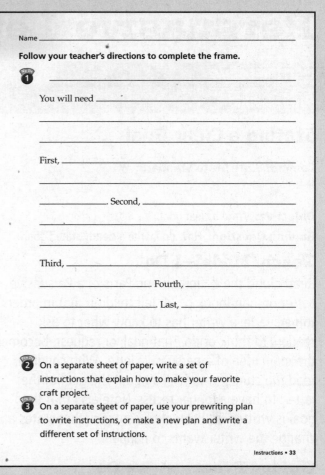

2 On a separate sheet of paper, write a set of instructions that explain how to make your favorite craft project.

3 On a separate sheet of paper, use your prewriting plan to write instructions, or make a new plan and write a different set of instructions.

✔ Corrective Feedback

IF . . . children have difficulty writing their instructions,

THEN . . . remind them to start by listing the things they would need for the activity. Tell them they can draw a picture of the activity to help them visualize the materials needed. Review that they need to write their steps in an order that makes sense. Encourage children to use time-order words to help them keep the steps in the correct order. Use the box on handbook p. 32 to review the transition words children can use.

Focus Trait: Word Choice

Explain to children that using vague words in instructions can confuse readers. Remind them to choose exact words so that readers can follow the steps. On the board, rewrite sentences from the model on handbook p. 32 so that the words are vague, such as *First, have **someone** cut **bread** into **pieces**. Spread the peanut butter on four of the squares.*

Discuss how vague words cause confusion. For example, a reader might not know who should cut the bread (an adult), which bread to cut (both slices), and how to cut it (into four squares). Have pairs read each others' instructions to make sure exact words are included.

Persuasive Letter

Minilesson 21

Stating a Clear Goal

Common Core State Standard: W.2.1

Objective: Write a clear goal.

Guiding Question: How do I write a clearly stated goal?

Teach/Model—I Do

Read aloud the definition and Parts of a Persuasive Letter on handbook p. 34. Tell children that in order to persuade, a writer has to know what to ask readers to think or do. That goal, or request, becomes the main idea of a persuasive letter. With children, read the student model. Point out the goal of the letter: to have a longer recess. Note also that the goal is written in a complete sentence that states a change the writer wants to happen.

Guided Practice—We Do

Together with children, brainstorm a list of changes they would like to see in class. Guide them to write each change in the form of a goal for a persuasive letter. For example, *Our class would like to do arts and crafts every Friday* or *Please allow us to choose our own books for reading hour.* Make sure that each goal is written as a complete sentence, and point out that each goal states a clear change to be made.

Practice/Apply—You Do

COLLABORATIVE Tell partners to make a list of 3 changes that they would like made to their school lunch or cafeteria services. Direct them to write each change in the form of a goal for a persuasive letter. Remind partners that each goal should be written as a full sentence.

INDEPENDENT Have children make a list of 3 changes they would like to see in their homes or communities. Ask them to write each change in the form of a goal for a persuasive letter.

Conference/Evaluate

Circulate as children write and help them think of goals. Remind them to write goals in complete sentences.

Minilesson 22

Drafting a Persuasive Letter

Common Core State Standards: W.2.1, L.2.2b

Objective: Write a persuasive letter.

Guiding Question: How do I draft a persuasive letter?

Teach/Model—I Do

Review the model on handbook p. 34. Direct children's attention to the body of the letter, noting the detailed reasons why the goal (more recess time) is important. Tell children that every detail that supports the goal makes the goal seem more reasonable and important. Point out all parts of the letter, including the use of commas in the greeting and closing.

Guided Practice—We Do

 Direct children to the frame on handbook p. 35. Guide them to suggest community changes they'd like to see happen. Choose one idea to use as the subject of the frame, such as *Our community needs to make changes to the hours of the public library.* Help children suggest detailed reasons that support the goal. Have them write in their books as you write on the board.

Practice/Apply—You Do

 COLLABORATIVE Direct children to Activity 2, suggesting that they use their school lunch goals from Minilesson 21 as a topic. Remind children to write their goal as a full sentence and to support it using detailed reasons. Encourage children to use all parts of a letter as they complete this frame.

 INDEPENDENT Have children read the directions. Tell them to use their prewriting plan from Lesson 11 or to brainstorm new ideas using Graphic Organizer 7.

Conference/Evaluate

During the writing process, circulate and offer encouragement and help as needed. Evaluate using the rubric on p. 104.

 Digital
- eBook
- WriteSmart
- Interactive Lessons

Persuasive Letter

A **persuasive letter** is addressed to a single reader. It makes a request and gives reasons for the request.

Parts of a Persuasive Letter

- Heading, greeting, body, closing, and signature
- A goal, or request
- Detailed reasons for the request
- An ending that ties things together

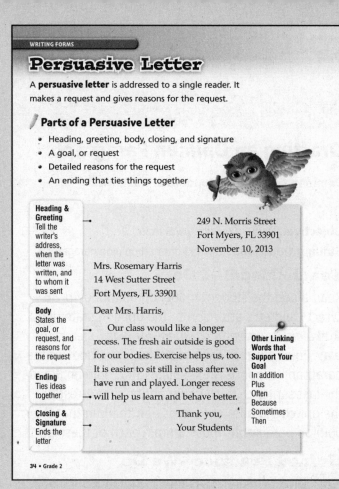

Heading & Greeting
Tell the writer's address, when the letter was written, and to whom it was sent

249 N. Morris Street
Fort Myers, FL 33901
November 10, 2013

Mrs. Rosemary Harris
14 West Sutter Street
Fort Myers, FL 33901

Body
States the goal, or request, and reasons for the request

Dear Mrs. Harris,

　　Our class would like a longer recess. The fresh air outside is good for our bodies. Exercise helps us, too. It is easier to sit still in class after we have run and played. Longer recess will help us learn and behave better.

Ending
Ties ideas together

Other Linking Words that Support Your Goal
In addition
Plus
Often
Because
Sometimes
Then

Closing & Signature
Ends the letter

Thank you,
Your Students

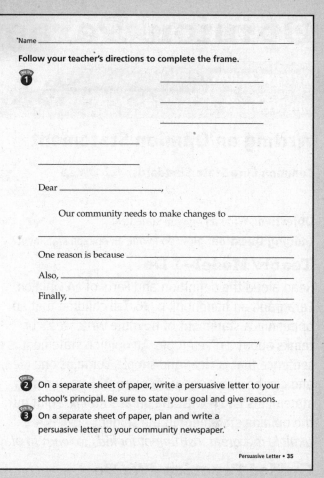

*Name _____

Follow your teacher's directions to complete the frame.

1

_____

_____

_____

_____

Dear _____,

　　Our community needs to make changes to _____

_____

One reason is because _____

Also, _____

Finally, _____

_____

_____

_____,

_____

2 On a separate sheet of paper, write a persuasive letter to your school's principal. Be sure to state your goal and give reasons.

3 On a separate sheet of paper, plan and write a persuasive letter to your community newspaper.

Corrective Feedback

IF . . . children are not supporting their goals with detailed reasons,

THEN . . . remind them to also consider what might occur if the goal of the letter is not met. Have children ask themselves, "What will happen if this change isn't made?" and make a list of answers that could support their goal. Encourage them to consider everyone who is affected by the existing problem and everyone who might benefit from the proposed change.

Focus Trait: Ideas

When children brainstorm topic ideas, encourage them to consider the following list of questions:

Who is this letter for, and what changes can that person make?

What changes would I like to see happen?

What changes might my friends like to see happen?

When children brainstorm body ideas, encourage them to consider this list of questions:

Why is this change necessary?

Who will benefit most from the change?

What problems will continue if the change is not made?

Opinion Paragraph

Minilesson 23

Writing an Opinion Statement

Common Core State Standards: W.2.1, W.2.5

Objective: Write an opinion statement.

Guiding Question: How do I write an opinion statement?

Teach/Model—I Do

Read aloud the definition and Parts of an Opinion Paragraph on handbook p. 36. Tell children that an opinion is a statement of how the writer feels or thinks about a given topic. An opinion statement is a sentence that is clear and simple, contains one idea, and can be supported with reasons. Some opinion statements begin with the phrase *I think*. Point out the opinion statement in the student model: *A ukulele is a great instrument for kids to learn to play.*

Guided Practice—We Do

On the board, write the following topics: food, books, and hobbies. With children, write one opinion statement for each topic. Include an unpopular or unexpected opinion, such as *The dictionary is the best book to read* or *I enjoy vegetables more than candy* to show children that an opinion may be unique to the writer.

Practice/Apply—You Do

COLLABORATIVE Have partners develop one more opinion statement for each topic on the board. Ask children to write statements that reflect their own feelings and thoughts about what they like or do not like.

INDEPENDENT Have children choose two new topics. Tell children to pick one topic they feel favorably about and one they do not. Ask them to write an opinion statement for each, showing their thoughts and feelings about what they like and dislike.

Conference/Evaluate

As children write, circulate and help them write their opinion statements. Remind children that the statement should be clear and simple and should reflect their feelings and thoughts.

Minilesson 24

Drafting an Opinion Paragraph

Common Core State Standards: W.2.1, W.2.5

Objective: Draft an opinion paragraph.

Guiding Question: How do I draft an opinion paragraph?

Teach/Model—I Do

Read aloud the student model on handbook p. 36. Direct children's attention to the opinion statement: *A ukulele is a great instrument for kids to learn to play.* Point out that each sentence in the body of the paragraph supports and explains that opinion. Read the last sentence to children, noting that it restates the opinion in different words. Tell children that their opinion paragraphs must contain each of these parts.

Guided Practice—We Do

 Direct children to Frame 1 on handbook p. 37. Together, write a topic sentence, such as *The drums are the most difficult instrument to play because you need a good sense of rhythm.* Guide children to give other reasons that support the opinion and to make sure to use all parts of an opinion paragraph. Have children write in their books as you write on the board.

Practice/Apply—You Do

 COLLABORATIVE Direct children to Frame 2, suggesting that they use their list of topics from the You Do section of Minilesson 23 to complete the frame. Remind children to write their opinion as a full sentence, to support their opinion using clear reasons, and to include all parts of an opinion paragraph.

 INDEPENDENT Tell children to use their prewriting plan from Lesson 12 or to brainstorm new ideas using Graphic Organizer 7.

Conference/Evaluate

During the writing process, circulate and offer encouragement and help as needed. Evaluate using the rubric on p. 104.

 Digital
• eBook
• WriteSmart
• Interactive Lessons

Opinion Paragraph

An **opinion paragraph** tells about an opinion, or the idea a writer has about something. It explains all of the reasons why the writer holds that opinion.

Parts of an Opinion Paragraph

- An opinion that uses clear words and shows how you feel about the topic
- Strong reasons that support and explain your opinion
- An ending that repeats your opinion, using different words

Opinion Tells what the writer thinks about a topic	A ukulele is a great instrument for kids to learn to play. It is a lot like a guitar, **only** smaller. That means it is easier for a kid to hold. A guitar has six strings, **but** a ukulele only has four. It is easier to play **because** there are fewer strings. The ukulele comes in lots of different shapes and colors. You can even get a red ukulele or one with your favorite picture painted on it. The **best** reason for learning how to play a ukulele is that you can show off your singing talents. I think every kid should learn how to play a ukulele.
Strong Reasons Explain why the writer feels that way	
Ending Repeats the opinion in different words	

Other Linking Words that Connect Opinions and Reasons
In addition
Plus
Often
Finally
And

Name _____

Follow your teacher's directions to complete Frames 1 and 2.

1 The drums are the most difficult instrument to play because _____

Another reason is because _____

_____. But _____

_____. Sometimes _____

_____

In my opinion, _____

_____

2 _____

_____. Also, _____

_____

_____. Another reason _____

_____. And so, _____

_____

3 On a separate sheet of paper, use your prewriting plan to write an opinion paragraph, or make a new plan to write about why it is important to try new things.

✓ Corrective Feedback

IF . . . children are writing to persuade,

THEN . . . remind them that an opinion paragraph should support their opinion using details and examples but shouldn't tell readers what to do. Show children the difference between opinion statements and goals, which are used in persuasive paragraphs. For example, *Opinion: A ukulele is a great instrument for kids to learn how to play. Goal: We should have ukulele classes at our school. Opinion: I enjoy vegetables more than candy. Goal: Eat vegetables instead of candy.*

Focus Trait: Voice

A writer's voice should reveal how he or she really sounds. Tell children that when writing an opinion piece, they need to use strong words that show their thoughts and feelings. Write these sentences on the board and have children practice writing opinion statements in their own voices. Answers will vary; possible answers are given.

I think summer is _____. (so boring, the best season of all)

If you have to choose between soccer and basketball, I think that _____. (soccer is better exercise, basketball is more of a blast)

I think gym class is _____. (the most exciting class, totally useless)

I think that computers are _____. (hard to use, fun to learn about)

Persuasive Paragraph

Minilesson 25	**Minilesson 26**

Stating a Goal

Common Core State Standard: W.2.1

Objective: State a goal or call to action.

Guiding Question: How can I state a goal?

Teach/Model—I Do

Explain to children that words such as *We should all* and *Let's work together* usually begin statements about something a person wants you to do or agree with. These words usually express more than an opinion. They state a goal, or a call to action. On the board, write *Start now to help Earth.* Then write *Don't waste water!* Point out the goal you want readers to agree with and the rule you've suggested to help achieve that goal.

Guided Practice—We Do

Guide children to think of 2 or 3 other goals related to helping Earth, such as *Save paper to save trees.* Help children state goals as complete sentences and suggest a rule to help reach the goal, such as *Always reuse scrap paper.*

Practice/Apply—You Do

COLLABORATIVE Tell partners to write 2 or 3 goals related to staying safe, such as *Wear a bike helmet.* Have partners state their goals as complete sentences and suggest one way to reach the goal. Remind them that goals should be clear and exact.

INDEPENDENT Have children brainstorm a goal they want their classmates to achieve, such as *Earn all As and Bs* or *Read 10 books this month.* Tell them to add rules or suggestions for how readers can achieve the goal.

Conference/Evaluate

Circulate and help children write their goals.

Drafting a Persuasive Paragraph

Common Core State Standard: W.2.1

Objective: Write persuasive text to support an opinion.

Guiding Question: How can I write a persuasive paragraph?

Teach/Model—I Do

Read the definition, Parts of a Persuasive Paragraph, and model on handbook p. 38. Point out that the model starts with an opinion and gives a goal and reasons and examples that explain the opinion. It uses transition words to keep ideas in order. Explain that persuasive writing often uses words such as *because* and *also* to link opinions to reasons.

Guided Practice—We Do

 Have children turn to handbook p. 39. For Frame 1, work with children to write an opinion sentence about year-round school. Guide them to support the opinion with reasons and examples to help complete the persuasive paragraph. Have children write in their books as you write on the board.

Practice/Apply—You Do

 COLLABORATIVE For Frame 2, have children work in small groups to write a paragraph on why there should, or should not, be school on Saturdays. Have groups share their paragraphs.

 INDEPENDENT Have children use their prewriting plan from Lesson 13 or brainstorm new ideas, using Graphic Organizer 15. Remind them to support their opinions.

Conference/Evaluate

During the writing process, circulate and offer encouragement and help as needed. Evaluate using the rubric on p. 104.

- eBook
- WriteSmart
- Interactive Lessons

Persuasive Paragraph

A **persuasive paragraph** gives your opinion. It tries to make your readers think or do something.

Parts of a Persuasive Paragraph

- A topic sentence that states your opinion
- Reasons why you feel that way
- Examples for the reasons
- An ending that tries to make your readers agree with you

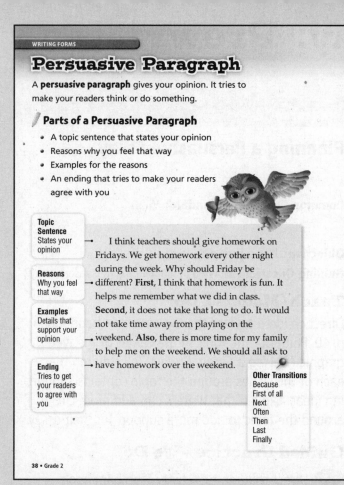

Topic Sentence
States your opinion

Reasons
Why you feel that way

Examples
Details that support your opinion

Ending
Tries to get your readers to agree with you

→ I think teachers should give homework on Fridays. We get homework every other night during the week. Why should Friday be different? **First**, I think that homework is fun. It helps me remember what we did in class. **Second**, it does not take that long to do. It would not take time away from playing on the weekend. **Also**, there is more time for my family to help me on the weekend. We should all ask to have homework over the weekend.

Other Transitions
Because
First of all
Next
Often
Then
Last
Finally

Name _____

Follow your teacher's directions to complete Frames 1 and 2.

1 I think that _____ First, _____

_____

Second, _____

_____

_____. Also, _____

_____

_____

2 We think that _____

_____ First of all, _____

_____

_____. Next, _____

_____

_____. Finally, _____

3 On a separate sheet of paper, use your prewriting plan to write a persuasive paragraph, or make a new plan to write a persuasive paragraph about school.

✓ Corrective Feedback

IF . . . children have difficulty organizing their persuasive paragraphs,

THEN . . . remind them to start by making a strong opinion statement that includes a goal. Encourage children to list reasons for the opinion, followed by examples. Help children restate their opinion in their closing. Use the box on handbook p. 38 to review other transition words they can use. Explain that these words can help them write their ideas in an order that makes sense.

Focus Trait: Word Choice

Explain to children that one way to improve writing is to get rid of words they use over and over again, such as *good, thing,* and *nice.* Remind them that replacing these overused words with more exact words will help express what they really think and feel. For example:

> *Jason's story was <u>nice</u>.*
> *Jason's story was so scary.*

Write the following sentences on the board. Have children rewrite them without the overused words.

> *Eating vegetables is <u>good.</u> (healthy)*
>
> *That is a great <u>thing</u>. (movie)*
>
> *What a <u>nice</u> cat! (gorgeous)*

Persuasive Essay: Prewriting

Minilesson 27

Selecting a Topic You Feel Strongly About

Common Core State Standard: W.2.1

Objective: Select a topic you feel strongly about.

Guiding Question: How do I choose a topic that I feel strongly about?

Teach/Model—I Do

Read aloud the definition and Parts of a Persuasive Essay on handbook p. 40. Explain to children that the goal of a persuasive essay is to encourage readers to take action or make a change. If a writer has many clear reasons why the reader should take action, then the writer feels strongly enough about the topic to write a good persuasive essay.

Guided Practice—We Do

Discuss with children a school rule they want to change. Guide them to state that topic as a goal. For example, *We should all wear school uniforms.* Write the goal on the board. Together, list as many reasons as possible as to why this change should be made. As a group, determine whether the topic is strong enough for a persuasive essay. Help children decide whether there are enough clear reasons to support the goal.

Practice/Apply—You Do

COLLABORATIVE Have partners think of two possible goals for a persuasive essay. Have them list as many supporting reasons as possible for each. Finally, have them choose and circle one goal as the best topic for a persuasive essay.

INDEPENDENT Have children think of one more possible goal for a persuasive essay. Ask them to list as many supporting reasons as possible and decide whether the goal would make a good persuasive essay.

Conference/Evaluate

Circulate, reminding children to ask themselves if the goal they chose has enough clear reasons.

Minilesson 28

Planning a Persuasive Essay

Common Core State Standard: W.2.1

Objective: Plan a persuasive essay.

Guiding Question: How do I plan a strong persuasive essay?

Teach/Model—I Do

Direct children toward the topic web on handbook p. 40. Point out the topic in the center of the web graphic (*Having a Safety Buddy*). Tell children that each of the circles around the topic contains supporting ideas. Explain that writers can add more circles around the topic to add more support for their essay.

Guided Practice—We Do

 Direct children to Activity 1 on handbook p. 41. As a group, choose one topic from the list. Then, together, draw a web on the board and fill it with supporting ideas for the selected topic. Each supporting reason should relate to the topic. For example, children might suggest *Keeps you healthy and strong* as a reason why *Eating fruits and vegetables* is important.

Practice/Apply—You Do

 COLLABORATIVE Direct children to Activity 2, suggesting that they choose their topic from the You Do section of Minilesson 27 or one of the other topics at the top of handbook p. 41 to complete the activity.

 INDEPENDENT Have children read the directions. Tell them to use their prewriting plan from Lesson 14 or to brainstorm new ideas using Graphic Organizer 15.

Conference/Evaluate

During the writing process, circulate and offer encouragement and help as needed. Evaluate using the rubric on p. 104.

Digital
- eBook
- WriteSmart
- Interactive Lessons

Persuasive Essay: Prewriting

A **persuasive essay** tells about a goal and explains why the goal is important.

Parts of a Persuasive Essay

- A beginning that states a clear goal, or something you want readers to do
- Middle paragraphs that tell reasons why the goal is important
- Facts that explain more about each reason
- An ending that states the goal in a different way

Brainstorming List

- Putting seat belts on school buses
- Learning how to swim
- Having a safety buddy
- Eating fruits and vegetables

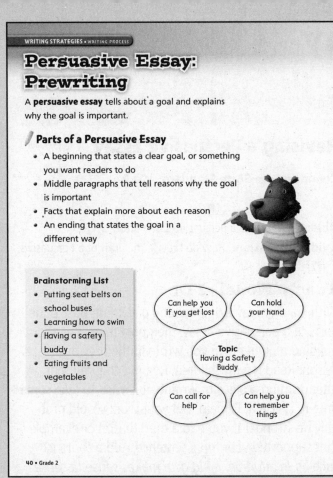

Topic
Having a Safety Buddy

- Can help you if you get lost
- Can hold your hand
- Can call for help
- Can help you to remember things

Name _____

Follow your teacher's directions to complete this page.

1 a.

Putting seat belts in school buses

Learning how to swim

Eating fruits and vegetables

Eating a good breakfast

Raising money for the local fire department

b.

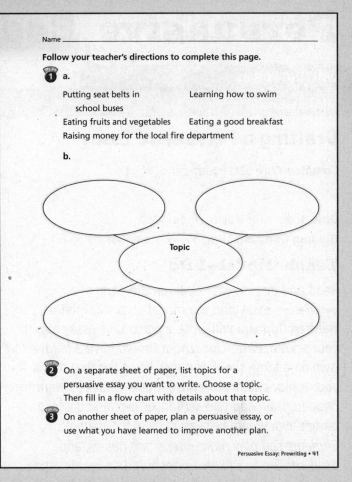

Topic

2 On a separate sheet of paper, list topics for a persuasive essay you want to write. Choose a topic. Then fill in a flow chart with details about that topic.

3 On another sheet of paper, plan a persuasive essay, or use what you have learned to improve another plan.

✓ Corrective Feedback

IF . . . children are having a hard time supporting their topics,

THEN . . . remind them to consider first what action they want readers to take. Then they should consider who would most benefit from the action. Children should consider the positive outcomes as well as the consequences of not taking action. Write this information on the board so that children can use it as supporting material in their graphic organizers.

Focus Trait: Ideas

To help children think of ideas for persuasive essay topics, have them make a list of people, places, and things that are important to them. Then, children should list possible changes related to those people, places, and things. Guide them to choose the topic for which they can think of a compelling change. Practice with children. For example:

What's Important to Me: my dog, riding bikes, my friends, art

Changes: dogs should be allowed in school; parents should buy me a new bike; my friends should come for a sleepover; we should have more art classes in school

Persuasive Essay

Minilesson 29

Drafting a Persuasive Essay

Common Core State Standard: W.2.1

Objective: Write a persuasive essay.

Guiding Question: How do I write a persuasive essay?

Teach/Model—I Do

Read and discuss with children the parts of a persuasive essay and the model on p. 42. Then tell children that you will write a persuasive essay about your school. Write *Our school should have a bigger gym* on a large sheet of paper. Point out that this is your topic sentence because it tells what you want to happen. Then add two sentences explaining why a bigger gym would be a good idea; for example, *Students can play more interesting games*, and *Students are less likely to get hurt*. Use words such as *because* and *for example*. Wrap up by restating the goal in a final sentence. Then point out the introduction, body, and conclusion.

Guided Practice—We Do

 Have children turn to Frame 1 on handbook p. 43. Ask them to complete the first sentence so it reads *Our school should let students dance during lunch*. Ask children to suggest reasons why this idea makes sense, such as *fun* and *physical fitness*. Write these reasons on the board as children copy them into their books. Guide children to write a strong concluding sentence. Read the completed essay with children and talk about how it persuades.

Practice/Apply—You Do

 COLLABORATIVE Have children work in pairs to write a persuasive essay for Activity 2.

 INDEPENDENT Have children write a persuasive essay for Activity 3.

Conference/Evaluate

Check that children use a topic sentence and give reasons and details in the body of the essay. Evaluate using the rubric on p. 104.

Minilesson 30

Revising a Persuasive Essay

Common Core State Standard: W.2.5

Objective: Revise a persuasive essay draft.

Guiding Question: How do I revise the draft of a persuasive essay?

Teach/Model—I Do

With children, review handbook p. 42. Emphasize the parts of a persuasive essay. Then post the essay about building a bigger gym you wrote in the previous lesson. Read it with children. Remind children that after drafting a piece of writing, it is wise to take some time to revise it. Explain that your work would probably be stronger if you had a third reason or example that supported your topic sentence. Add a sentence such as *In addition, a big gym makes sense because the whole school could fit inside it for assemblies*. Replace one or two words as well, such as changing *have* to *build* in the opening sentence. Read the revised essay aloud and review the changes with children.

Guided Practice—We Do

Reread the essay children wrote for Frame 1 on handbook p. 43. Guide children to make 3–4 small revisions to make the essay clearer, more exact, or more persuasive. Have children make changes in their books; if time permits, have them make a clean copy on another sheet of paper.

Practice/Apply—You Do

COLLABORATIVE Have pairs revise the work they did on Activity 2 in the previous minilesson.

INDEPENDENT Have children reread and revise the persuasive essays they wrote for Activity 3 in the previous minilesson.

Conference/Evaluate

Ask children to show you what revisions they are making and explain why they think these changes will improve their essays.

 Digital • eBook • WriteSmart • Interactive Lessons

Persuasive Essay

A **persuasive essay** names a clear goal and explains why the goal is important. It also shows ways the reader can reach that goal.

Parts of a Persuasive Essay

- An introduction that includes a clear goal
- A body that gives reasons why the goal is important
- Facts that tell more about each reason
- A conclusion that restates the goal

Introduction
Includes a clear and important goal

Body
Shows why the goal is important

Facts
Tell more about each reason

Conclusion
Repeats the goal using different words

Having a buddy around is a lot of fun. But having a buddy is most important because a buddy can keep you safe.

Safety buddies can help you if you get lost **because** your buddy might know exactly where you are. **Also**, one buddy can get help from a teacher or parent if the other buddy is in trouble. And two buddies can remember more than one buddy. That can help you to avoid trouble, **too**.

Everyone should have a safety buddy with them at all times. It can help you stay safe and have fun!

Other Linking Words that Support Your Goal
In addition
Often
Finally
Then
For example

Name _____

Follow your teacher's directions to complete the frame.

1 Our school should _____

The most important reason _____

_____. For example, _____

It is good because _____

Then, kids can _____

I think _____

2 On a separate sheet of paper, write a persuasive essay to your school's principal. Include all of the parts of a persuasive essay.

3 On a separate sheet of paper, use your prewriting plan to write a persuasive essay, or plan and write a persuasive essay about exercising before going to bed at night.

Corrective Feedback

IF . . . children are struggling to find revisions,

THEN . . . encourage them to use a revision checklist. Have them consider these questions:

Does my essay have a topic sentence that states the goal? Do all of my reasons relate back to the goal? Do I use facts to tell more about each reason? Are my words exact and colorful? Did I place sentences in an order that makes sense? Do I end by restating the goal in different words?

Focus Trait: Organization

Remind children that a well-organized essay has sentences in a logical order. On the board, write:

Fruits and vegetables keep you healthy.

Everyone should eat fruits and vegetables.

Oranges have vitamins that keep you from getting sick. Fruits and vegetables taste great. Fruits and vegetables give you energy.

Have children find the topic sentence and place that first. Then ask children to place the supporting details in an order that makes sense.

Everyone should eat fruits and vegetables.

*Fruits and vegetables keep you healthy. **For example**, oranges have vitamins that keep you from getting sick. **Also,** fruits and vegetables give you energy. **Finally,** they taste great!*

Fictional Narrative Paragraph

Minilesson 31

Using Time-Order Words to Help Sequence

Common Core State Standard: W.2.3

Objective: Use time-order words to help sequence.

Guiding Question: How do I use time-order words to show the order of events in a narrative?

Teach/Model—I Do

Read aloud and discuss handbook p. 44. Point out that a narrative paragraph shows action, or a series of events that occur in time-order. Read the time-related words in the student model: *Today, first, then,* and *finally.* Then, point out the order of action in the model: Mark puts on the shirt, then the sweater, then the tie. Time-order words help writers to put the action in the correct sequence, or order, so the story makes sense to the reader.

Guided Practice—We Do

With children's help, write on the board a list of time-order words, such as *last, after, soon,* and *next.* Then, guide children to brainstorm the sequence of action they take when they arrive at school. Help children add the correct time-order words. Example: *First, we go into the classroom. Then, we find our desks. Next, we unpack our backpacks. Finally, we get out our homework.*

Practice/Apply—You Do

COLLABORATIVE In small groups, children should write the list of steps involved in making a sandwich. Ask children to use time-order words that support the correct order of the steps.

INDEPENDENT Have each child list the steps they take at the end of the school day. Have children include time-order words to show sequence of action.

Conference/Evaluate

Circulate, reminding children that time-order words relate to the sequence of action: the first action should be written first and should use time-order words such as *first* or *in the beginning.*

Minilesson 32

Drafting a Fictional Narrative Paragraph

Common Core State Standard: W.2.3

Objective: Draft a fictional narrative paragraph.

Guiding Question: How do I draft a fictional narrative paragraph?

Teach/Model—I Do

With children, review Parts of a Fictional Narrative Paragraph on handbook p. 44. Point out the beginning, middle, and ending in the student model. Direct children to the Kinds of Details box and the bold-faced details in the model. Explain that all narratives are rich in details that relate to the senses.

Guided Practice—We Do

 Direct children to Frame 1 on handbook p. 45. Guide them to complete the first sentence. For example, …*First, we saw the big stack of gifts that our family had given her.* As children volunteer sentences for the rest of the frame, guide them to include details about the characters and settings. Have children write in their books as you write on chart paper.

Practice/Apply—You Do

 COLLABORATIVE Ask children to work in small groups to complete Frame 2 using a classroom event or activity as the subject. Remind them that because this is a fictional paragraph, they should make up the events and details in the story. Encourage them to add details that relate to the senses.

 INDEPENDENT Have children read the directions. Tell them to use their prewriting plan from Lesson 16 or to brainstorm new ideas using Graphic Organizer 10.

Conference/Evaluate

During the writing process, circulate and offer encouragement and help as needed. Evaluate using the rubric on p. 104.

 Digital
- eBook
- WriteSmart
- Interactive Lessons

Fictional Narrative Paragraph

A **fictional narrative paragraph** is a short story that a writer has made up. It has a clear beginning and ending.

Parts of a Fictional Narrative Paragraph

- A beginning sentence that introduces the characters and setting
- Details that tell more about the characters and setting
- Action that tells what is happening

Beginning Sentence
Introduces the characters and setting

Details
Tell about the characters and setting

Action
Puts events in time order

→ Mark's favorite thing to do in his playroom is to dress up. Today, Mark has decided to dress up as his Daddy, who is Mark's favorite person. First, Mark picks out the **biggest** shirt that he can find in Daddy's closet. Then, he puts on a **warm**, **blue** sweater that comes down to his knees. Wearing Daddy's clothes makes Mark feel **silly** and **happy** at the same time. But his costume isn't finished yet. Finally, he puts on Daddy's **orange** and **purple** tie. Perfect!

Kinds of Details
Colors
Shapes
Sizes
Sounds
Feelings
Actions

Name _____

Follow your teacher's directions to complete Frames 1 and 2.

1 We had a great time at my dog's surprise party. First, we saw

_____

In the next room, we heard _____

_____. We played

_____. Then we all ate _____

_____

The best part of the party was _____

_____

2 _____

_____. Next,

_____. We saw _____

_____. Finally, _____

_____

_____

_____

3 On a separate sheet of paper, use your prewriting plan to write a fictional narrative paragraph, or make a new plan to write about a holiday parade.

✓ Corrective Feedback

IF . . . children are not including enough details,

THEN . . . have them list the important characters, places, and objects in their fictional narrative paragraphs and then write sense words related to each. Remind them that sense words describe things we see, touch, smell, taste, and hear. Practice with your completed Frame 1. For example: *my dog: curly brown hair, big smile. Music: loud, exciting. Birthday cake: sweet smell, sticky frosting, rich chocolate.* Children can add these sense words to their narratives.

Focus Trait: Ideas

To help children choose an idea for their fictional narrative paragraph, guide them to think of and list as many events as possible. They can be realistic or make-believe. For example:

Going to the park

Helping to make dinner

Traveling to the moon

Have children choose the event that most interests them and make up characters, settings, and descriptions that relate to the event. Encourage them to enjoy using their imaginations.

Fictional Narrative Paragraph

Minilesson 33

Revising a Fictional Narrative Paragraph

Common Core State Standard: W.2.3

Objective: Revise a fictional narrative paragraph.

Guiding Question: How do I revise the draft of a fictional narrative paragraph?

Teach/Model—I Do

Read handbook p. 46. Tell children that revising a draft means making changes to improve the writing. Revising may include adding descriptions and dialogue. Point out how descriptions and dialogue in the model help the reader imagine the story.

Guided Practice—We Do

Display the writing you did on chart paper for Frame 1 on handbook p. 45. Tell children to revise the fictional narrative paragraph on a separate sheet of paper. Tell them to add more description and some dialogue such as, *"Turning two was the best day of my life,"* said my dog.

Practice/Apply—You Do

COLLABORATIVE Direct children to their work on Frame 2 on handbook p. 45. Have partners work together to add dialogue and descriptions to the narrative paragraph. Encourage them to make at least three changes to the draft.

INDEPENDENT Have children revise their drafts from Activity 3 on handbook p. 45. Encourage them to add dialogue and descriptions and make sure their ideas are clear and interesting.

Conference/Evaluate

Circulate as children revise. Help them determine where they can add dialogue and description.

Minilesson 34

Publishing a Fictional Narrative Paragraph

Common Core State Standard: W.2.3

Objective: Publish a fictional narrative paragraph.

Guiding Question: How do I prepare a fictional narrative paragraph for publishing?

Teach/Model—I Do

Tell children that preparing a work for publishing means creating a work that is neat and ready for a reader. Direct children to the model on handbook p. 46. Point out that, when using dialogue, a new paragraph is begun each time a character speaks. A finished work that is ready for publishing will be neatly written and have paragraphs that are indented.

Guided Practice—We Do

 Direct children to Frame 1 on handbook p. 47. Together, come up with a first sentence, such as *It was my first time painting a portrait.* Work with children to complete the rest of the frame. Children should write in their books as you write on the board. Next, guide children to add paragraph breaks after characters speak, such as after the second sentence. On a separate sheet of paper, children should rewrite the frame in neat handwriting with the correct indentations.

Practice/Apply—You Do

 COLLABORATIVE Direct children to Frame 2. Ask partners to write a fictional narrative paragraph with dialogue and correct indentations. Have children rewrite their paragraphs neatly to prepare them for publication.

 INDEPENDENT Have children complete Activity 3. Remind them to use their best handwriting to create a work that is ready for publication. Have them share with the class.

Conference/Evaluate

Circulate and offer encouragement and help as needed. Evaluate using the rubric on p. 104.

 Digital
- eBook
- WriteSmart
- Interactive Lessons

Fictional Narrative Paragraph

A **fictional narrative paragraph** is a short story that has a clear beginning and end. It can seem like a true story, but it is a made up story.

Parts of a Fictional Narrative Paragraph

- Details that describe the characters, setting, and events
- Dialogue that shows what characters are like and the exact words they say
- Events told in an order that makes sense

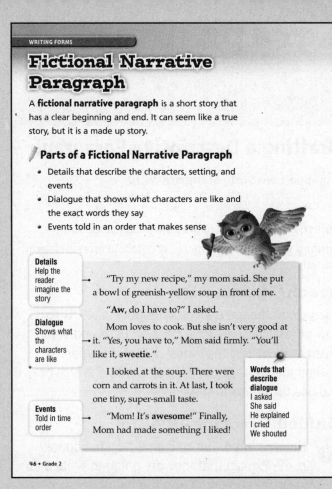

Details
Help the reader imagine the story

Dialogue
Shows what the characters are like

Events
Told in time order

"Try my new recipe," my mom said. She put a bowl of greenish-yellow soup in front of me.

"**Aw**, do I have to?" I asked.

Mom loves to cook. But she isn't very good at it. "Yes, you have to," Mom said firmly. "You'll like it, **sweetie**."

I looked at the soup. There were corn and carrots in it. At last, I took one tiny, super-small taste.

"Mom! It's **awesome**!" Finally, Mom had made something I liked!

Words that describe dialogue
I asked
She said
He explained
I cried
We shouted

46 • Grade 2

Name _____

Follow your teacher's directions to complete Frames 1 and 2.

1 It was my first time _____

My teacher began, saying, " _____
_____"

It was hard. I told her, " _____
_____"

Finally, _____
_____
_____. My teacher smiled and said," _____
_____"

2 _____
_____
_____. Next, _____
_____
_____. In the end, _____
_____

We all said, " _____"

3 On a separate sheet of paper, use your prewriting plan to write a fictional narrative paragraph, or make a new plan to write about trying something new for the first time.

Fictional Narrative Paragraph • 47

Corrective Feedback

IF . . . children are struggling to write dialogue,

THEN . . . have them work in pairs or groups to act out their stories. Tell them to imagine they are the characters in the story. What would the characters say? How would they say it? Remind them that dialogue should sound like real people talking, so it is okay to write ideas much like the way they would speak.

Focus Traits: Voice

Remind children that voice should match their purpose. Since their purpose is to narrate, or tell a story, they should use a voice that sounds natural as if they are telling a story to their friends. Write:

Tina's family went to the beach. The weather was hot. They enjoyed the beach. The waves felt good.

Have children help you rewrite the sentences in a more natural voice.

Example:

Tina's family went to the beach. It was awesome! Jumping in the cool waves felt great because it was a hot day.

Grade 2 • 47

Descriptive Paragraph

Minilesson 35

Brainstorming Sensory Details

Common Core State Standard: W.2.2

Objective: Write a descriptive paragraph with a main idea and supporting details.

Guiding Question: How can I create word pictures for my readers?

Teach/Model—I Do

Read aloud the definition, parts, and model on handbook p. 48. Point out the boldfaced words in the model, such as *giant* and *soft green.* Tell children that these kinds of words and phrases are called *sense words.* Explain that sense words help create pictures in a reader's mind. They can help readers share the writer's experiences of seeing, hearing, touching, smelling, and tasting things.

Guided Practice—We Do

With children, identify other examples of sense words (boldfaced) in the model. Then help children write additional sense words about the park by guiding them to complete the following sentences: *I hear___; I see___; I taste___; I smell___; I . touch___.*

Practice/Apply—You Do

COLLABORATIVE Tell partners to create word pictures about a farm, such as *old red barn.* If they wish, children can use the sentence frames from the We Do activity above. Invite children to share their sentences.

INDEPENDENT Have children create word pictures about a winter day. They may wish to use the sentence frames from the We Do activity above. Invite children to share their word pictures when they are done.

Conference/Evaluate

Circulate and help children with their sentences. Remind them that sense words create a word picture.

Minilesson 36

Drafting a Descriptive Paragraph

Common Core State Standard: W.2.2

Objective: Write a descriptive paragraph to express ideas.

Guiding Question: How can I use details to express ideas in a descriptive paragraph?

Teach/Model—I Do

Read aloud the material on handbook p. 48. Discuss how phrases such as *little chirping birds* and *soft green lawn* helped the writer describe the park. Review the *Some Color, Shape, and Size Words* box, and use the words in sentences.

Guided Practice—We Do

 Have children turn to Frame 1 on handbook p. 49. Explain that they are going to write a descriptive paragraph about a fun place, such as a water park. Guide children to choose a place and work with them to create a topic sentence. Then guide children to use their senses to describe the place, using the words in parentheses as cues. Add an illustration if you wish and have children do the same. Have children write in their books as you write on the board.

Practice/Apply—You Do

 COLLABORATIVE For Frame 2, have partners write a new paragraph about a place. Remind children to include sense words in their descriptions. Have partners share their responses.

 INDEPENDENT Have children read the directions. Tell them to use their prewriting plan from Lesson 18 or brainstorm new ideas, using Graphic Organizer 15.

Conference/Evaluate

During the writing process, circulate and offer encouragement and help as needed. Evaluate using the rubric on p. 104.

 Digital
- eBook
- WriteSmart
- Interactive Lessons

Descriptive Paragraph

A **descriptive paragraph** uses sense words to tell about a person, place, or thing.

Parts of a Descriptive Paragraph

- A topic sentence that tells what is being described
- Details that tell what you see, hear, feel, smell, and sometimes taste
- Words that describe color, shape, and size

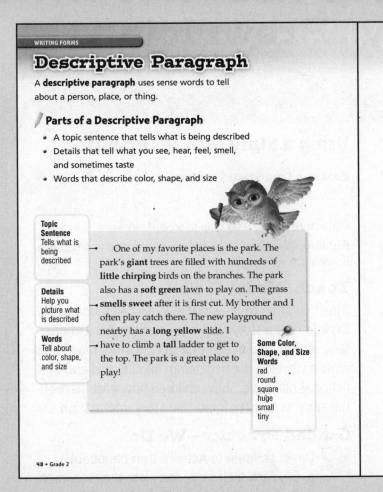

Topic Sentence
Tells what is being described

Details
Help you picture what is described

Words
Tell about color, shape, and size

→ One of my favorite places is the park. The park's **giant** trees are filled with hundreds of **little chirping** birds on the branches. The park also has a **soft green** lawn to play on. The grass → **smells sweet** after it is first cut. My brother and I often play catch there. The new playground nearby has a **long yellow** slide. I → have to climb a **tall** ladder to get to the top. The park is a great place to play!

Some Color, Shape, and Size Words
red
round
square
huge
small
tiny

Name _____

Follow your teacher's directions to complete Frames 1 and 2.

1   A fun place is _____

(see) _____

(hear) _____.

(smell) _____

_____ (feel)

_____

_____. That is why the _____

_____ is a fun place!

2   _____

_____ (see) _____

_____ (hear) _____

(smell) _____

(feel) _____

3   On a sheet of paper, use your prewriting plan to write a descriptive paragraph. If you like, make a new plan to write about a place near your home.

✔ Corrective Feedback

IF . . . children have difficulty including sense words in their paragraphs,

THEN . . . once they choose their topic, they should ask themselves, *What do I see? What do I hear? What do I feel? What do I taste?* and *What do I smell?* Encourage children to ask and answer these questions as they write their descriptions.

Focus Trait: Word Choice

Tell children that they can write clearer descriptions by making comparisons. Explain that a simile is a comparison that uses the words *like* or *as*. Practice with a sentence in the model on handbook p. 48.

On the board, write,

The park's giant trees are filled with hundreds of birds chirping like little bells.

Discuss how the simile paints a clear picture of the scene. Guide children to volunteer similes for other descriptions in the model, such as *soft green lawn (the green lawn felt soft as a cloud)* and *long yellow slide (a long slide that is as bright and yellow as the sun)*.

Fictional Story: Prewriting

Minilesson 37

Choosing Characters and a Setting

Common Core State Standard: W.2.3

Objective: Choose characters and a setting.

Guiding Question: How do I choose characters and a setting for a fictional story?

Teach/Model—I Do

Read aloud the Parts of a Fictional Story on handbook p. 50. Tell children that an exciting story includes a character that has a problem to solve or a challenge to overcome. A writer will choose a setting that fits the character and situation. Point out that Max and Molly's first problem was figuring out who was yelling outside the window. A logical setting for the story was Max and Molly's living room and outside.

Guided Practice—We Do

On the board, write the following situation: *A character looking for something that is lost.* With children, brainstorm a list of characters who might find themselves in this situation: *a pirate looking for treasure, a neighbor looking for a lost dog, a big brother looking for his little sister, a dog looking for a bone.* Then, guide them to brainstorm a logical setting for each scenario.

Practice/Apply—You Do

COLLABORATIVE Have partners consider the following situation: *A character overcoming a fear.* Ask them to list three possible characters who might find themselves in this situation, and then brainstorm a logical setting for each character's scenario.

INDEPENDENT Have children brainstorm two characters, each with a different problem to solve. Then, have children brainstorm a logical setting for each.

Conference/Evaluate

Circulate as children write and help them come up with ideas. Remind children that an exciting story revolves around a character that has a problem to solve.

Minilesson 38

Using a Story Map to Organize

Common Core State Standard: W.2.3

Objective: Use a story map to organize ideas.

Guiding Question: How do I use a story map to organize a fictional story?

Teach/Model—I Do

Direct children to the story map on handbook p. 50. Explain that a story map is an outline of the characters, setting, and action in a story. A story map helps writers develop the beginning, middle, and end of a fictional narrative. Show children how each part of the story map gives important story information.

Guided Practice—We Do

 Direct children to Activity 1 on handbook p. 51. With their help, complete the story map on the board, asking children to complete the map in their books. Point out that an exciting story contains a problem that has to be solved. Ask children to brainstorm problems that Jacob might face in the middle of the story. For example, ask, *Should Jacob open the door or should Jacob stay in the spooky cabin? Why do you think Jacob's dog is barking?* Together, complete the story map by resolving the problem in the story.

Practice/Apply—You Do

 COLLABORATIVE Direct pairs to Activity 2. Remind them to consider a challenge that characters must overcome and a logical setting for the narrative.

INDEPENDENT Have children read the directions. Tell them to use their prewriting plan from Lesson 19 or brainstorm new ideas using Graphic Organizer 11.

Conference/Evaluate

During the writing process, circulate and offer encouragement and help as needed. Evaluate using the rubric on p. 104.

- eBook
- WriteSmart
- Interactive Lessons

Fictional Story: Prewriting

A **fictional story** is made up. It has characters, a plot, and a setting.

Parts of a Fictional Story

- A beginning, middle, and ending
- A plot with a problem that gets solved
- Action told in time order
- Dialogue, or words spoken by the characters

Brainstorming List

- Mrs. Lee's bird comes to visit
- Chef Primo burns the dinner
- A day at the zoo
- Taking care of Simba the cat

Title: When Mrs. Lee's Bird Came to Visit

Setting	Characters
the living room	Max and Molly
outside	Mom
	Mrs. Lee and her bird
Plot	

Beginning

Max and Molly hear someone outside yelling for a cookie.

Middle

It is a bird that is yelling. The bird belongs to Mrs. Lee.

End

Max and Molly return the bird.

Name _____

Follow your teacher's directions to complete this page.

 1

Setting	Characters
A spooky cabin in the woods	Jacob and his dog
Plot	

Beginning

Jacob's dog starts barking loudly at the front door.

Middle

End

2 Choose one group of characters for a fictional story. Then, on a separate piece of paper, fill in a story map to plan your story.

A stray dog and cat	Three ladybugs
A dad and his two children	Two best friends
Two brothers	Lightning and thunder

3 On another sheet of paper, plan a fictional story, or use what you have learned to improve another plan.

✓ Corrective Feedback

IF . . . children are struggling to think of characters and problems,

THEN . . . suggest that they brainstorm settings first. Have them list places they find interesting: *a magic castle, the field of championship soccer game, an amusement park.* Then, have them think of problems that might occur in these places and characters that might face these problems.

Focus Trait: Organization

Tell children that stories are organized to help the reader understand and enjoy the writing. On the board, write following:

Beginning: characters, setting, background information

Middle: the problem or challenge

Ending: the solution to the problem, or the end of the challenge

Once they have the basic structure of the story planned, encourage children to follow their story maps to complete a draft.

Fictional Story

Writing Story Dialogue

Common Core State Standards: W.2.3, L.2.2

Objective: Write simple dialogue.

Guiding Question: How do I write dialogue?

Teach/Model—I Do

Read aloud the model on handbook p. 52 and point out the following sentences: *Molly said, "Mom, look. That bird keeps saying it wants a cookie."* Explain that the writer used quotation marks to show Molly's exact words. The writer also used the word *said* and a comma to separate Molly's exact words from the other parts of the sentence. On the board write *"Let's get going!" yelled Paul.* Tell children that an exclamation point or question mark can sometimes be used instead of a comma to separate a speaker's exact words from the rest of the sentence.

Guided Practice—We Do

Guide children to create sentences about a pet they have or would like to own. Record their sentences on the board, using and reinforcing dialogue form. For example, *"My cat does silly things," said Kayla.* Encourage children to dictate the placement of end punctuation and quotation marks.

Practice/Apply—You Do

COLLABORATIVE Tell small groups to take turns saying sentences while other group members record the sentences as dialogue. Remind groups to include quotation marks and end punctuation and to add the speaker's name.

INDEPENDENT Write several sentences on the board and have children rewrite them as dialogue.

Conference/Evaluate

Circulate, noting which children are writing in correct dialogue form. Help others as needed.

Drafting a Fictional Story

Common Core State Standard: W.2.3

Objective: Write a fictional narrative.

Guiding Question: How do I write a good story?

Teach/Model—I Do

Read aloud the information on handbook p. 52. Tell children that a story has a beginning, a middle, and an ending. It also has characters, a setting, and a plot with a problem to be solved. Often, a story has dialogue to show the exact words a character says.

Guided Practice—We Do

 Have children turn to the frame on handbook p. 53. Explain that they are going to write a story. Draw children's attention to the dialogue shown at the beginning. Then guide them to suggest ideas and then sentences for the middle and end of the story. Encourage children to use dialogue. Have children write in their books as you write on the board.

Practice/Apply—You Do

 COLLABORATIVE For Activity 2, have small groups write a fictional story about a new pet. Suggest that they use their sentences from the Guided Practice of Minilesson 39 as inspiration. Remind them to write a beginning, a middle with events told in order, and an ending. Have groups share their stories.

 INDEPENDENT Have children read the directions. Tell them to use their prewriting plan from Lesson 20 or to brainstorm new ideas, using Graphic Organizer 4. Encourage children to use at least one line of dialogue.

Conference/Evaluate

During the writing process, circulate and offer encouragement and help as needed. Evaluate using the rubric on p. 104.

Digital
• eBook
• WriteSmart
• Interactive Lessons

Fictional Story

A **fictional story** is made up and tells what happens to one or more characters. It also has a setting and a plot.

Parts of a Fictional Story

- A beginning, a middle, and an ending
- A plot with a problem that gets solved
- Events told in time order
- Dialogue, or words spoken by the characters, in quotation marks

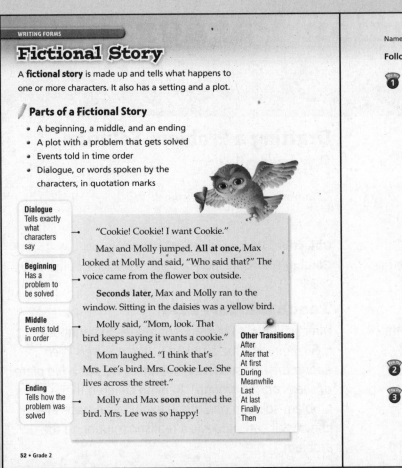

Dialogue
Tells exactly what characters say

Beginning
Has a problem to be solved

Middle
Events told in order

Ending
Tells how the problem was solved

"Cookie! Cookie! I want Cookie."

Max and Molly jumped. **All at once**, Max looked at Molly and said, "Who said that?" The voice came from the flower box outside.

Seconds later, Max and Molly ran to the window. Sitting in the daisies was a yellow bird.

Molly said, "Mom, look. That bird keeps saying it wants a cookie."

Mom laughed. "I think that's Mrs. Lee's bird. Mrs. Cookie Lee. She lives across the street."

Molly and Max **soon** returned the bird. Mrs. Lee was so happy!

Other Transitions
After
After that
At first
During
Meanwhile
Last
At last
Finally
Then

Name _____

Follow your teacher's directions to complete the frame.

 1 "I want to go to the zoo today," said Lucy. _____

_____. All at once, _____

_____

Seconds later, _____

_____

"_____," said _____

_____. At first, _____

_____

_____. Then _____

_____

_____. At last, _____

_____

 2 On a sheet of paper, write a fictional story about a new pet.

3 On a sheet of paper, use your prewriting plan to write a fictional story. If you like, make a new plan to write a story about a hero.

✓ Corrective Feedback

IF . . . children have difficulty including dialogue in their stories or do not write it correctly,

THEN . . . remind them that dialogue is a way to show the exact words a character says. Have children choose an event from their stories. Work together to rewrite part of the event as dialogue. Use the model on handbook p. 52 to review the different ways to write dialogue.

✏ Focus Trait: Organization

Remind children that stories have a beginning, middle, and ending. During the revision stage, have partners read each others' stories to make sure they are organized well. On the board, write these questions to guide peer revision:

Does the beginning clearly describe the characters and setting? Is any background information missing?

Does the middle give events in time order? Is a problem or challenge introduced?

Does the ending solve the problem? Does the story feel complete?

Problem-Solution Paragraph

Minilesson 41

Determining a Problem and a Solution

Common Core State Standard: W.2.2

Objective: Determine a problem and a solution.

Guiding Question: How do I choose a topic for a problem-solution paragraph?

Teach/Model—I Do

Read and discuss handbook p. 54. Tell children that good writers choose topics that they know and understand. Suggest that children consider issues that they see or experience every day.

Guided Practice—We Do

On the board, write the following areas in which a solvable problem might be found: *Home, School, Community*. Then, with children's help, identify one problem in each area, such as *Home: We create too much garbage every week. School: Students don't have enough time in the library. Community: The playground in the park needs repairs.* Together, list one possible solution for each problem.

Practice/Apply—You Do

COLLABORATIVE Have partners brainstorm another problem for each of the three areas above. Then, have them list a possible solution for each problem.

INDEPENDENT Have children brainstorm two new problems of their choice. Then ask them to list possible solutions for each problem. Finally, tell children to choose one problem-solution topic that they could use as the main idea of a problem-solution paragraph.

Conference/Evaluate

Circulate as children write and help them brainstorm ideas. Remind them that a problem-solution paragraph should be based on a topic they know and understand well.

Minilesson 42

Drafting a Problem-Solution Paragraph

Common Core State Standard: W.2.2

Objective: Draft a problem-solution paragraph.

Guiding Question: How do I draft a problem-solution paragraph?

Teach/Model—I Do

Direct children to the student model on handbook p. 54. Point out the problem (...*the squirrels keep eating the bird seed*) and solution (*We put a big plate of seeds on the ground*). Remind children that a problem-solution paragraph explores an issue they know well and suggests a realistic solution to the problem.

Guided Practice—We Do

 Direct children to Frame 1 on handbook p. 55. Guide them to identify the problem (a messy bedroom). With children's help, complete the first sentence. Example: *A messy bedroom is a problem because it can be hard to find things.* Together, complete the frame on the board. Have children write in their books as you write on the board.

Practice/Apply—You Do

 COLLABORATIVE Direct partners to Frame 2. Ask them to complete the frame using a problem that they know well and that has a realistic solution. Have partners share their writing.

 INDEPENDENT Have children read the directions. Tell them to use their prewriting plan from Lesson 21 or brainstorm new ideas using Graphic Organizer 12.

Conference/Evaluate

During the writing process, circulate and offer encouragement and help as needed. Evaluate using the rubric on p. 104.

Digital
- eBook
- WriteSmart
- Interactive Lessons

Problem-Solution Paragraph

A **problem-solution paragraph** describes a problem.
Then it tells how to fix the problem.

Parts of a Problem-Solution Paragraph

- A problem that needs to be fixed
- Details that explain the whole problem
- A way to solve the problem

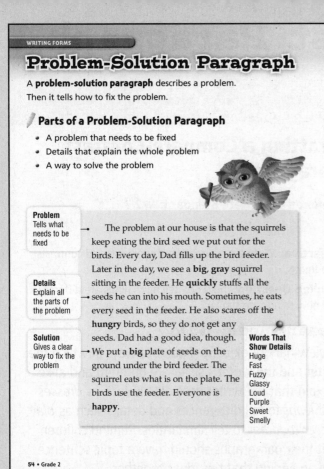

Problem
Tells what needs to be fixed

Details
Explain all the parts of the problem

Solution
Gives a clear way to fix the problem

The problem at our house is that the squirrels keep eating the bird seed we put out for the birds. Every day, Dad fills up the bird feeder. Later in the day, we see a **big, gray** squirrel sitting in the feeder. He **quickly** stuffs all the seeds he can into his mouth. Sometimes, he eats every seed in the feeder. He also scares off the **hungry** birds, so they do not get any seeds. Dad had a good idea, though. We put a **big** plate of seeds on the ground under the bird feeder. The squirrel eats what is on the plate. The birds use the feeder. Everyone is **happy**.

Words That Show Details
Huge
Fast
Fuzzy
Glassy
Loud
Purple
Sweet
Smelly

Name _____

Follow your teacher's directions to complete Frames 1 and 2.

1 A messy bedroom is a problem because _____
_____. It is a big problem when _____
_____
One quick way to fix the problem is _____
_____
That way, _____
_____

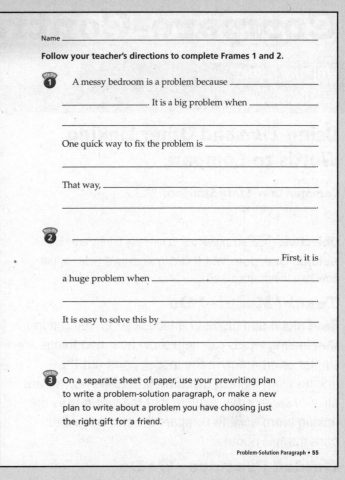
2 _____
_____. First, it is
a huge problem when _____
_____
It is easy to solve this by _____
_____

3 On a separate sheet of paper, use your prewriting plan to write a problem-solution paragraph, or make a new plan to write about a problem you have choosing just the right gift for a friend.

✓ Corrective Feedback

IF . . . children are unable to think of solvable problems,

THEN . . . suggest that they begin with a problem that affects them in a small way, such as a routine that needs to be changed or a habit that needs to be broken. Encourage them to use a graphic organizer, such as a web, to brainstorm a problem and solutions.

Focus Trait: Word Choice

Remind children that one way to help create a picture for the reader is to use descriptive words. Adjectives are words that describe how a person, place, or thing looks, feels, tastes, smells, and sounds. On the board, write:

Sight: large

Touch: bumpy

Taste: bitter

Smell: smoky

Sound: quiet

Ask children to suggest additional adjectives for each sense. Then encourage them to add adjectives to their paragraphs to better communicate the problem and its solution.

Compare-Contrast Paragraph

Using *Like* and Other Linking Words to Compare

Common Core State Standard: W.2.2

Objective: Use linking words to tell how things are similar.

Guiding Question: Which linking words will help me tell how two things are alike?

Teach/Model—I Do

Read aloud and discuss handbook p. 56. Tell children that linking words can help show how two things are similar or different. In the model, point out the linking word *alike* in this sentence: *However, we are* alike *in some ways.* Explain that the writer uses the linking word *alike* to compare the two people the paragraph is about.

Guided Practice—We Do

On the board, write these linking words: *like, both, same, also, too, alike.* Work with children to write a sentence that compares two people, animals, places, or things. Guide them to use one of the linking words from the board in the sentence. For example, you may give children a frame such as _____ *and* _____ *both have* _____.

Practice/Apply—You Do

COLLABORATIVE Have pairs write a sentence that compares two people, animals, places, or things. Instruct them to use a linking word such as *same* or *like* to clearly show similarities. Have them share what they have written.

INDEPENDENT Have children write a sentence that compares two people, animals, places, or things. Tell them to use a linking word to compare the two things they write about.

Conference/Evaluate

Have children share their sentences with you to make sure they compare two subjects using an appropriate linking word.

Drafting a Compare-Contrast Paragraph

Common Core State Standard: W.2.2

Objective: Write a paragraph that compares and contrasts two things.

Guiding Question: How do I tell how things are different and how things are similar?

Teach/Model—I Do

Review handbook p. 56. Point out ways in which the writer and the writer's sister are different and alike. Explain that the writer uses details such as *dresses* and *jeans* to tell differences and details such as *play soccer together* to tell similarities. Remind children that their paragraphs should have a topic sentence and an ending that ties ideas together.

Guided Practice—We Do

 1 Direct children to the frame on handbook p. 57. Tell them that together you will write a paragraph to compare and contrast two people, animals, places, or things. Help them draft a topic sentence such as *Fun Land and Splashdown Water Park are very alike.* Then, together, complete the frame with details that tell similarities and differences. Have children write in their books as you write on the board.

Practice/Apply—You Do

 2 **COLLABORATIVE** Have pairs plan and complete Activity 2. Tell children that they can choose two classmates, teachers, politicians, writers, inventors, athletes, and so on. Have pairs share what they have written.

 3 **INDEPENDENT** Have children read and follow the directions. Tell them to use their prewriting plan from Lesson 22 or to brainstorm a new plan using Graphic Organizer 14.

Conference/Evaluate

As children draft, have them evaluate their work using the rubric on p. 104.

Digital
• eBook
• WriteSmart
• Interactive Lessons

Compare-Contrast Paragraph

A **compare-contrast paragraph** tells how things are different and how they are alike. The subjects can be people, animals, places, or things.

Parts of a Compare-Contrast Paragraph

- A topic sentence that states the main idea
- Sentences that tell how things are different and how they are similar
- Details that help tell differences and similarities
- An ending that ties ideas together

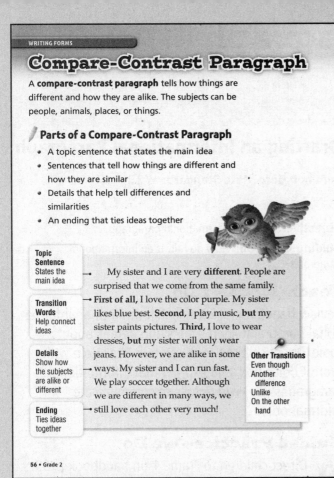

Topic Sentence
States the main idea

Transition Words
Help connect ideas

Details
Show how the subjects are alike or different

Ending
Ties ideas together

My sister and I are very **different**. People are surprised that we come from the same family. **First of all,** I love the color purple. My sister likes blue best. **Second,** I play music, **but** my sister paints pictures. **Third,** I love to wear dresses, **but** my sister will only wear jeans. However, we are alike in some ways. My sister and I can run fast. We play soccer together. Although we are different in many ways, we still love each other very much!

Other Transitions
Even though
Another difference
Unlike
On the other hand

Name _____

Follow your teacher's directions to complete the frame.

1 _____ and _____ are very alike. _____

First of all, _____

Second, _____

_____

_____

_____. Third, _____

_____

On the other hand, they are different, too. _____

_____

_____

_____

_____

_____

2 On a separate sheet of paper, write a paragraph that compares and contrasts two people you know.

3 Use your prewriting plan to write a compare-contrast paragraph, or make a new plan to write a paragraph that compares and contrasts two games.

✓ Corrective Feedback

IF . . . children have difficulty writing their compare-contrast paragraphs,

THEN . . . encourage them to make lists of how the two subjects are the same and different. Suggest that they use a Venn diagram to plan and organize their ideas.

Focus Trait: Organization

Explain that all of the details in a compare-contrast paragraph must tell about the main idea. Point out that details about how two subjects are alike are grouped together. Details about how two subjects are different are also grouped together. This helps readers understand the paragraph.

On the board, write these sentences about parrots and puffins:

1. Parrots and puffins are birds.
2. Parrots are colorful.
3. Puffins are black, white, and gray.
4. Both have beaks.

Have children group together sentences that tell how parrots and puffins are alike (1, 4) and how they are different (2, 3).

Informational Paragraph

Minilesson 45

Paraphrasing Information

Common Core State Standard: W.2.2

Objective: Paraphrase information.

Guiding Question: How do I paraphrase material I have read for an informational paragraph?

Teach/Model—I Do

Read aloud handbook p. 58. Tell children that *paraphrasing* means restating something you read using your own words instead of the original author's words. When writing an informational paragraph, writers often paraphrase words they have read.

Guided Practice—We Do

With children's help, paraphrase the definition of an informational paragraph at the top of handbook p. 58. Write the paraphrased definition on the board and guide children to compare the original text to the text written in the class's own words. For example: *An informational paragraph gives facts about people, places, and things.* Show children how paraphrasing may require adding and changing words or phrases until the new version makes sense to them.

Practice/Apply—You Do

COLLABORATIVE Have partners paraphrase the bulleted list on handbook p. 58. Suggest that children add bullets by breaking the existing bullet points into smaller parts. For example, the third bullet point might be broken into *Facts that give information about the topic* and *Facts and details put in logical order.* Have children share their final list with a neighboring group.

INDEPENDENT Have children paraphrase the first three sentences of the model on handbook p. 58. Challenge them to make the passage shorter rather than longer, without compromising the information.

Conference/Evaluate

Circulate as children write. Encourage them to use their own words by covering up the original passage and challenging them to use their powers of recall.

Minilesson 46

Drafting an Informational Paragraph

Common Core State Standard: W.2.2

Objective: Draft an informational paragraph.

Guiding Question: How do I draft an informational paragraph?

Teach/Model—I Do

Review handbook p. 58. Tell children that an informational paragraph shares facts and details about a topic. Direct children to the Details That Help with Word Choice box, and explain that informational paragraphs use vivid details to communicate information.

Guided Practice—We Do

 Direct children to Frame 1 on handbook p. 59. Guide them to complete the frame, asking them to write in their books as you write on the board. Encourage children to offer vivid details, such as the size of a suitcase or the manner in which to pack items into it. Tell them that the more details they use, the more successful a reader will be if they use this information to pack for a vacation.

Practice/Apply—You Do

 COLLABORATIVE Direct small groups to Frame 2. Tell them to choose a topic they know well, such as planting seeds for a garden or what to do if you cut yourself, and remind them to use many details in their writing.

 INDEPENDENT Have children read the directions. Tell them to use their prewriting plan from Lesson 23 or to brainstorm new ideas using Graphic Organizer 15.

Conference/Evaluate

During the writing process, circulate and offer encouragement and help as needed. Evaluate using the rubric on p. 104.

Digital
- eBook
- WriteSmart
- Interactive Lessons

Informational Paragraph

An **informational paragraph** tells facts and details about a person, place, or thing.

Parts of an Informational Paragraph

- An interesting topic sentence that tells the main idea
- Details that support and explain the main topic
- Facts that are told in an order that makes sense

Topic Sentence
Tells the main idea, or topic

Details
Support and explain the main idea

Order
Presents facts and details in a way that makes sense

Making a play toy for a cat is very easy. First, cut a **rectangle** out of a piece of cloth. Fold the rectangle in half to make a **square**. Next, use fabric glue along two edges. Leave the third edge open. When the glue dries, stuff catnip inside the square until it is **full** and **round**. Catnip is a plant that cats just **love**. Glue the last edge to shut the square. Finally, when it is all dry, give it to your cat. You will have a **happy** cat to play with!

Details that Help With Word Choice
Sounds
Shapes
Textures
Sights
Smells

Name _____

Follow your teacher's directions to complete Frames 1 and 2.

It is easy to pack a bag for a vacation or sleepover. First, _____ _____. Then, get out _____ After that, pack _____ _____. Always remember to _____ _____ Finally, _____ _____

_____ _____. When this happens, _____ Then, _____ Finally, _____ _____ _____

3 On a separate sheet of paper, use your prewriting plan to write an informational paragraph, or make a new plan to write about a craft project.

Corrective Feedback

IF . . . children are having difficulty paraphrasing source material,

THEN . . . remind them that they must understand the original material before they can paraphrase it. Suggest that they re-read the material. Then, encourage them to set aside the original and relate the material as they understand it to a partner. Finally, challenge children to write down what they understand, using their own language and without consulting the original.

Focus Trait: Ideas

Remind children that using synonyms is an important part of paraphrasing. Synonyms can also help clarify complicated information in their paragraphs.

On the board, write the following definition and examples:

Synonym: two words that mean the same thing

Big : Large   *Happy : Glad*

Fast : Quick   *Wet : Damp*

Little : Small   *Sugary : Sweet*

Tart : Sour   *Loud : Ear-splitting*

Thin : Skinny   *Rough : Scratchy*

Encourage children to use synonyms to avoid repetition as they write. Have children add to the list of synonyms above.

Research Report: Prewriting

Narrowing a Research Topic

Common Core State Standard: W.2.2

Objective: Brainstorm and choose a topic.

Guiding Question: How do I brainstorm and choose a topic for a research report?

Teach/Model—I Do

Read aloud handbook p. 60. Tell children that a good research topic is interesting to the writer and focuses on specific ideas about a subject. Point out that the writer started with a subject that was too broad to cover in a research report, *Animals*. Explain that this author narrowed down the subject until it focused on a specific topic, *Chipmunks*.

Guided Practice—We Do

Guide children to list subjects they are interested in researching, such as *sports*, *inventions*, and *countries*. Write their suggestions on the board. Together, choose one subject and guide children to narrow it until it is a specific topic. Draw an inverted triangle on the board and help children fill it with increasingly specific topics. For example, *sports→water sports→surfing→who invented surfing* or *countries→countries in North America→Canada→Ontario→city of Toronto*.

Practice/Apply—You Do

COLLABORATIVE Have partners choose two other topics from the board and narrow each until they are specific enough for a research report. Have them use an inverted triangle to organize their ideas as they narrow topics.

INDEPENDENT Have children brainstorm a topic of their choice and narrow it until it is a specific research topic.

Conference/Evaluate

Circulate as children write. Remind them that though they don't want their topic to be too broad, it also shouldn't be too specific to research.

Notetaking

Common Core State Standard: W.2.2

Objective: Organize ideas by taking notes.

Guiding Question: How do I take notes for a research report?

Teach/Model—I Do

Review Parts of a Research Report on handbook p. 60. Tell children that, as they do research for a report, they need to write down details that help them remember the information they have read. This is called *taking notes*. Explain that notes are short bits of information that do not have to be in sentence form. Direct children to the note cards on p. 60, and point out that each piece of information is a note the writer took about chipmunks.

Guided Practice—We Do

 Have children turn to Activity 1 on p. 61. Draw the inverted triangle on the board. Guide children to narrow from *animals→ mammals→rodents→groundhogs*. Then, help children research and write details about groundhogs on note cards. Have children write in their books as you write on the board.

Practice/Apply—You Do

 COLLABORATIVE Have pairs complete Activity 2 about a type of dinosaur, such as a stegosaurus. Provide them with source material to take their notes.

 INDEPENDENT Have children complete Activity 3 about another animal, using source material to help them take notes.

Conference/Evaluate

During the writing process, circulate and offer encouragement and help as needed. Evaluate using the rubric on p. 104.

 Digital
• eBook
• WriteSmart
• Interactive Lessons

Research Report: Prewriting

A **research report** tells facts and information about a topic. It has an introduction, a body, and a conclusion.

Parts of a Research Report

- An interesting introduction, or topic sentence, that names the main idea
- A body with facts and details about the topic
- Illustrations, when helpful
- A conclusion that wraps up the report

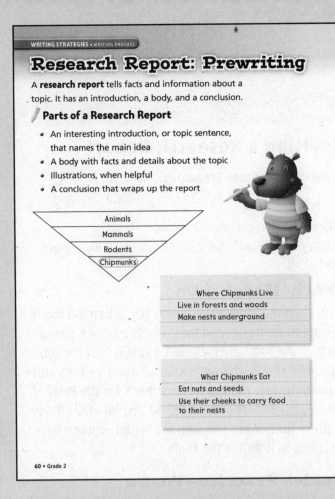

```
Animals
Mammals
Rodents
Chipmunks
```

Where Chipmunks Live
Live in forests and woods
Make nests underground

What Chipmunks Eat
Eat nuts and seeds
Use their cheeks to carry food
to their nests

Name _____

Follow your teacher's directions to complete this page.

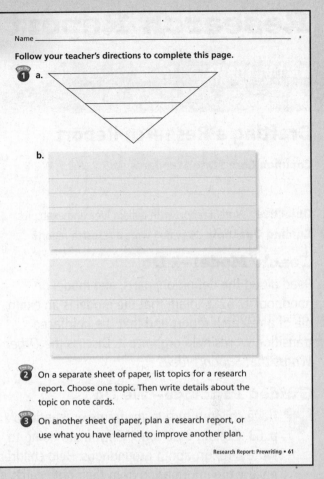

1 a.

b.

2 On a separate sheet of paper, list topics for a research report. Choose one topic. Then write details about the topic on note cards.

3 On another sheet of paper, plan a research report, or use what you have learned to improve another plan.

Corrective Feedback

IF . . . children are having difficulty creating notes,

THEN . . . remind them that they must understand the original material before they can recreate it as a note. Suggest first that they re-read the material. Then, have children set aside the original and write the material as a note in their own words. Have children ask partners if they understand the note.

Focus Trait: Ideas

Remind children that ideas for research reports come from asking questions about the topic. On the board, write:

Who?

What?

Where?

When?

Why?

How?

Suggest that children ask questions about their topic beginning with the words above. Questions that cannot be answered should be researched.

Research Report

Minilesson 49

Drafting a Research Report

Common Core State Standards: W.2.2, W.2.7, W.2.8

Objective: Write a report with a main idea and examples.

Guiding Question: How do I write a research report?

Teach/Model—I Do

Read aloud the definition, parts, and model on handbook p. 62. Explain that the model is an example of a research report and that the boldfaced transition words help organize it. Discuss the *Other Words that Support Ideas.*

Guided Practice—We Do

 1 Have children turn to the frame on handbook p. 63. Explain that, together, you are going to write a report about groundhogs. Help children review the information from their note cards on p. 61. Then write the report together. Have children write in their books as you write on the board. Leave the report on the board for use in Minilesson 50.

Practice/Apply—You Do

 2 **COLLABORATIVE** Have children read the directions. Ask small groups to work together to write a research report on a stegosaurus or any other dinosaur. They can use their note cards from handbook p. 61. Remind children to write an interesting introduction, a topic sentence, a body with facts that support the topic, and a conclusion that ties ideas together.

 3 **INDEPENDENT** Have children read the directions. Tell them to use their note cards from handbook p. 61 or to brainstorm new ideas using Graphic Organizer 4.

Conference/Evaluate

During the writing process, circulate and offer encouragement and help as needed. Evaluate using the rubric on p. 104.

Minilesson 50

Revising a Research Report

Common Core State Standards: W.2.7, W.2.8

Objective: Revise a research report.

Guiding Question: What can I do to improve my research report draft?

Teach/Model—I Do

With children, review handbook p. 62. Remind them that good writers revise their drafts to make sure all parts of the form are included. Explain that the rubric on p. 104 shows characteristics of good writing. Have children review the model and check for the Parts of a Research Report listed on p. 62. Explain that if any of these parts were missing, the writer would make revisions to improve the draft.

Guided Practice—We Do

Direct children to the frame on handbook p. 63. Together, locate the parts of a research report in the draft. Ask questions such as, *Is there an interesting opening and a topic sentence? Are facts and details well organized? Does the conclusion sum up the report?* Make changes on the board as children work in their books.

Practice/Apply—You Do

COLLABORATIVE Have partners revise their draft from Activity 2. Remind them to use the Parts of a Research Report and the rubric on p. 104 to guide their work.

INDEPENDENT Have children revise their draft from Activity 3. Tell them to use the rubric on p. 104 to help make changes.

Conference/Evaluate

Circulate and help children improve their writing. Evaluate using the rubric on p. 104.

 Digital
- eBook
- WriteSmart
- Interactive Lessons

Research Report

A **research report** gives information about a topic. It is written in your own words.

Parts of a Research Report

- An interesting opening that tells what the report is about
- A topic sentence that states the main idea
- Facts and details about the main idea
- Illustrations when useful
- A closing that sums up the report

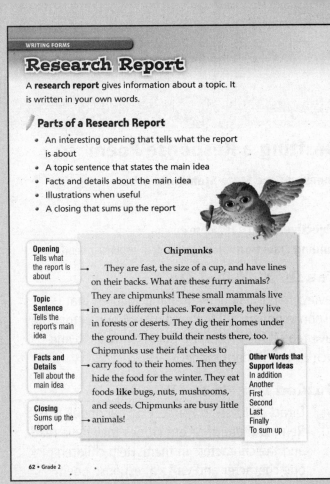

Opening
Tells what the report is about

Topic Sentence
Tells the report's main idea

Facts and Details
Tell about the main idea

Closing
Sums up the report

Chipmunks

They are fast, the size of a cup, and have lines on their backs. What are these furry animals? They are chipmunks! These small mammals live in many different places. **For example**, they live in forests or deserts. They dig their homes under the ground. They build their nests there, too. Chipmunks use their fat cheeks to carry food to their homes. Then they hide the food for the winter. They eat foods **like** bugs, nuts, mushrooms, and seeds. Chipmunks are busy little animals!

Other Words that Support Ideas
In addition
Another
First
Second
Last
Finally
To sum up

62 • Grade 2

Name _____

Follow your teacher's directions to complete the frame.

 1 Did you know that groundhogs are a kind of squirrel?

_____

_____

_____

_____ . For example, _____

_____ . In addition, _____

_____

_____

_____ . Another example is _____

_____

_____

_____

_____

2 On a separate sheet of paper, write a research report about a stegosaurus, or any other dinosaur.

3 On a separate sheet of paper, use your prewriting plan to write a research report. If you like, make a new plan to write a research report about a different animal.

Research Report • 63

Corrective Feedback

IF . . . children have difficulty organizing their research reports,

THEN . . . remind them to start each paragraph with a topic sentence that has one main idea. Tell them to write only the facts that tell about that main idea in the paragraph. Use the box on handbook p. 62 to review transition words that can help children keep their ideas in order.

Focus Trait: Voice

Explain that when writing a research report, children cannot use the exact words of others. They need to rewrite information in their own words. Write these sentences on the board and have children suggest ways to rewrite them:

The animal buries food in a hidden burrow below the ground.

The chipmunk sleeps in the old nest and is hidden from sight.

Some animals can hide out in the open because they are the same color as the places where they live.

Animals that hibernate in the winter stay asleep without eating and wake up in the spring.

Grade 2 • **63**

Response Poem

Minilesson 51

Drafting Free-Verse Poetry

Common Core State Standard: W.2.1

Objective: Draft a free-verse poem.

Guiding Question: How do I write a free-verse poem?

Teach/Model—I Do

Read aloud handbook p. 64. Tell children that many poems have rhyme and rhythm, such as the student model; other poems—called *free-verse poems*—have neither rhyme nor regular rhythm pattern. A free-verse poem is usually about one topic, such as a moment in time or something special. Each line can offer a specific detail that describes the topic.

Guided Practice—We Do

On the board, write the title *Outside*. With children's help, write six brief descriptions of an ideal outdoor setting. For example, *The moon glows like a light bulb in the sky. The air feels fresh and cool on my face. I smell hot dogs and hamburgers on the grill,* and so on. Encourage children to consider the sights, sounds, and feelings they might experience outdoors. Guide children to arrange the descriptions into a six-line free-verse poem. Be sure to limit each line to one simple idea.

Practice/Apply—You Do

COLLABORATIVE Have partners brainstorm a topic for writing. Then ask children to list six details, one for each line, that describe the topic they chose. Have them arrange their ideas into a six-line poem. Remind them that the poem should not rhyme.

INDEPENDENT Have children write a free verse poem. Encourage children to write about a special moment or person. Ask them to include the sights, sounds, and feelings associated with that time or person.

Conference/Evaluate

Circulate as children write. Remind them that each line should address a specific detail related to the topic and that the poem should not rhyme.

Minilesson 52

Drafting a Response Poem

Common Core State Standard: W.2.1

Objective: Draft a response poem.

Guiding Question: How do I draft a response poem?

Teach/Model—I Do

Review handbook p. 64. Remind children that response poems tell their feelings about a story they have read. Many response poems include rhyme, such as the student model.

Guided Practice—We Do

 Direct children to Frame 1 on handbook p. 65. Remind them of recent stories they have read and the characters in them. Help children pick one character and write a response poem about him or her. Guide them to notice each end rhyme and create lines that reflect the character truthfully and end with the words provided. Have children write in their books as you write on the board.

Practice/Apply—You Do

 COLLABORATIVE Direct small groups to Frame 2. Remind children of the settings in stories they have recently read. Have groups choose one setting and write a response poem about it. Tell them to make each pair of lines rhyme as they did in Frame 1. Allow groups to complete the frame and share their drafts when they have finished.

 INDEPENDENT Have children read the directions. Tell them to use their prewriting plan from Lesson 26 or to brainstorm new ideas using Graphic Organizer 15.

Conference/Evaluate

During the writing process, circulate and offer encouragement and help as needed. Evaluate using the rubric on p. 104.

 • eBook • WriteSmart • Interactive Lessons

Response Poem

A **response poem** can be about a story. It can also be about the way that a story made you think or feel.

Parts of a Response Poem

- Lines that may or may not rhyme
- Sensory words that describe the way things look, sound, taste, smell, or feel
- A musical beat, or rhythm

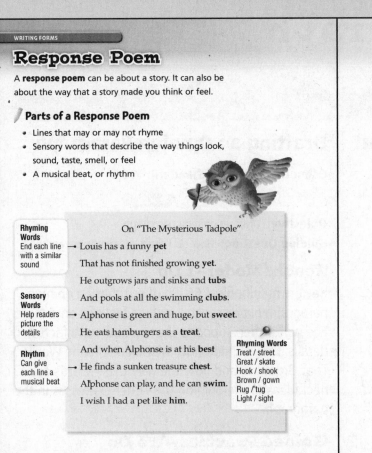

Rhyming Words
End each line with a similar sound

Sensory Words
Help readers picture the details

Rhythm
Can give each line a musical beat

On "The Mysterious Tadpole"

Louis has a funny **pet**

That has not finished growing **yet.**

He outgrows jars and sinks and **tubs**

And pools at all the swimming **clubs.**

Alphonse is green and huge, but **sweet.**

He eats hamburgers as a **treat.**

And when Alphonse is at his **best**

He finds a sunken treasure **chest.**

Alphonse can play, and he can **swim.**

I wish I had a pet like **him.**

Rhyming Words
Treat / street
Great / skate
Hook / shook
Brown / gown
Rug / tug
Light / sight

Name _____

Follow your teacher's directions to complete Frames 1 and 2.

1 My Favorite Character: _____

_____ kind.

_____ mind.

_____ wear.

_____ hair.

_____ goes.

_____ shows.

2

_____ bright.

_____ see.

_____ stay.

3 On a separate sheet of paper, use your prewriting plan to write a response poem, or make a new plan to write a response poem about your favorite book.

Corrective Feedback

IF . . . children struggle with rhyme,

THEN . . . remind them that rhyme is when two words end with the same sound, like *moon* and *soon*. Suggest that children begin by creating a word bank of words that describe or relate to their topic. Then, ask them to pair a rhyming word with each word in their bank. From this collection, children can form lines that end with these word pairs.

Focus Trait: Word Choice

Explain to children that poems are very concise works: they say much with very few words. It is important, therefore, to choose words that are vivid and interesting. Remind children that words that describe emotions and the senses convey meaning to readers. On the board, write:

I saw the chipmunk run.

He sat in the sun.

I watched the silly chipmunk race.

He sat on leaves in a sunny place.

Point out to children vivid words, such as *silly, race,* and *sunny*. Suggest that they add vivid sense words to their poems to add interest.

Opinion Paragraph

Minilesson 53

Providing a Concluding Statement

Common Core State Standard: W.2.1

Objective: Provide a concluding statement in an opinion paragraph.

Guiding Question: How do I write a concluding statement in an opinion paragraph?

Teach/Model—I Do

Read aloud handbook p. 66. Explain to children that a concluding statement repeats the main idea of an opinion paragraph, using different words. Read the topic sentence in the student model, *The playground near the public library is in bad shape.* Then read the concluding statement, *We need to ask adults to rebuild the playground.* Point out that both statements are about the bad condition of the playground.

Guided Practice—We Do

On the board, write the following topic sentence of an opinion paragraph: *The invention of the telephone changed the world.* With children, brainstorm a statement that might conclude this opinion paragraph, such as *When the telephone came into our lives, everything got better.* Explain to children that new information should not be included in a closing statement.

Practice/Apply—You Do

COLLABORATIVE Supply children with a few topic sentences, such as *Dogs are very smart pets.* Ask children to write a closing statement for an opinion paragraph about the topic.

INDEPENDENT Ask children to write a closing statement for an opinion paragraph about another topic, such as *Oranges are the best fruit.*

Conference/Evaluate

Circulate as children write and help them draft concluding statements that use different words from the topic statement.

Minilesson 54

Drafting an Opinion Paragraph

Common Core State Standard: W.2.1

Objective: Draft an opinion paragraph.

Guiding Question: How do I draft an opinion paragraph?

Teach/Model—I Do

Review handbook p. 66. Point out that an opinion paragraph expresses the writer's feelings on a topic. The writer then supports that opinion with facts and details. Direct children to the box of Linking Words That Organize, and note the way these words connect ideas to the opinion the writer expresses in the paragraph.

Guided Practice—We Do

 Direct children to the frame on handbook p. 67. Before writing, brainstorm with children qualities that make a good friend. Then, with children, complete the frame. Have children write in their books as you write on the board. As you write, point out the meaning of linking words that help organize the paragraph.

Practice/Apply—You Do

 COLLABORATIVE Direct partners to Activity 2. Remind children of the parts of an opinion paragraph before they begin. Have partners complete the activity and share their drafts when they have finished.

 INDEPENDENT Have children read the directions. Tell them to use their prewriting plan from Lesson 27 or to brainstorm new ideas using Graphic Organizer 15.

Conference/Evaluate

During the writing process, circulate and offer encouragement and help as needed. Evaluate using the rubric on p. 104.

 Digital
• eBook
• WriteSmart
• Interactive Lessons

Opinion Paragraph

An **opinion paragraph** states an opinion, or the way a writer feels about something. It then supports the opinion with facts and details.

Parts of an Opinion Paragraph

- A topic sentence that clearly states an opinion
- Facts, examples, and reasons that support the opinion
- Details that make the opinion clearer to the reader
- Linking words that organize the paragraph and connect ideas
- Ending sentence that repeats the opinion in different words

Topic Sentence
States the writer's opinion

Facts, Examples, and Reasons
Support the writer's opinion

Details
Describe the opinion

The playground near the public library is in bad shape. A few of the climbing structures are breaking. The red plastic is peeling off the stairs, **and** that makes them slippery. Even the old gate is broken. That means little kids can leave the playground when their parents are not watching. It was a fun park to play in, **but** now no one goes there because it is too old. We need to ask adults to rebuild the playground.

Other Linking Words that Organize
So that
Then
Also
In addition
Besides

Name _____

Follow your teacher's directions to complete the frame.

1 I am a good friend because _____

_____

In addition, I _____

_____. Also _____

_____. Because

I am a good friend, _____

_____

Then, _____

_____

Besides, _____

_____

_____. Most importantly, _____

_____

2 On a separate sheet of paper, write an opinion paragraph about your favorite sport.

3 On a separate sheet of paper, use your prewriting plan to write an opinion paragraph, or make a new plan to write about a change you would like to see in your neighborhood.

Corrective Feedback

IF . . . children struggle with concluding statements,

THEN . . . remind them that the concluding statement shares the same idea and opinion as the topic sentence but uses different words. Suggest that children draft a concluding sentence that begins with one of these sentence openers:

I feel that...

I think...

In my opinion...

Focus Trait: Organization

Good writers organize their paragraphs to help readers understand their ideas. One kind of organization is to put the most important details before all of the others. On the board, write:

Topic sentence: _____

Detail 1:

Detail 2:

Detail 3:

Ask children to fill in the outline, placing the most convincing or important detail first. Suggest that children use this outline as they draft their opinion paragraphs.

Story Response Paragraph

Minilesson 55

Writing Story Titles

Common Core State Standard: W.2.1

Objective: Write story titles.

Guiding Question: How do I write a title in a story response paragraph?

Teach/Model—I Do

Read aloud handbook p. 68. Point out the title and author's name in the student model. Explain to children that including the title and author in a response paragraph tells readers which work the paragraph is about. It also gives credit for writing to the author. Both of these details—the title and the author's name—are important parts of a story response paragraph.

Guided Practice—We Do

With children's help, write on the board a title and author of a story the children recently read, such as _I read The Dog That Dug for Dinosaurs by Shirley Raye Redmond._ Underline the title, and explain to children that underlining titles of books and putting titles of short stories or poems in quotation marks are ways to draw attention to the title and to separate it from the rest of the writer's words.

Practice/Apply—You Do

COLLABORATIVE Have partners choose a title and author of a work they have recently read. Ask them to incorporate it into a sentence like the one on the board from the We Do section. Ask groups to share their work to check for understanding.

INDEPENDENT Have children write a sentence stating a response to, or opinion of, a story they have read. Ask children to include the title and author's name in that statement.

Conference/Evaluate

Circulate and help children brainstorm the titles and authors of works they have recently read.

Minilesson 56

Drafting a Story Response Paragraph

Common Core State Standard: W.2.1

Objective: Draft a story response paragraph.

Guiding Question: How do I draft a story response paragraph?

Teach/Model—I Do

Review handbook p. 68. Remind children that response paragraphs tell readers what the writer thought of a story or part of a story. Point out the main idea in the topic sentence of the student model: that the dog in The Dog That Dug for Dinosaurs was very smart. Explain to children that the words in the Words that Link Ideas box connect details and examples from the story to the writer's response.

Guided Practice—We Do

 Direct children to Frame 1 on handbook p. 69. Remind them of recent stories they have read. With children, complete the frame, paying attention to the Words that Link Ideas.

Practice/Apply—You Do

 COLLABORATIVE Direct partners to Frame 2. Have them complete the frame with a response to another story they have read. Remind partners to include the title and author in their response, as they did in Minilesson 55.

 INDEPENDENT Have children read the directions. Tell them to use their prewriting plan from Lesson 28 or to brainstorm new ideas using Graphic Organizer 7.

Conference/Evaluate

During the writing process, circulate and offer encouragement and help as needed. Evaluate using the rubric on p. 104.

 Digital
• eBook
• WriteSmart
• Interactive Lessons

Story Response Paragraph

A **story response paragraph** tells what the writer thinks and feels about a story. The details in the paragraph support the writer's opinion.

Parts of a Story Response Paragraph

- A topic sentence that clearly states an opinion
- Details and examples from the story that support the opinion
- Linking words that organize the paragraph and connect ideas
- A clear ending that states the writer's topic in a different way

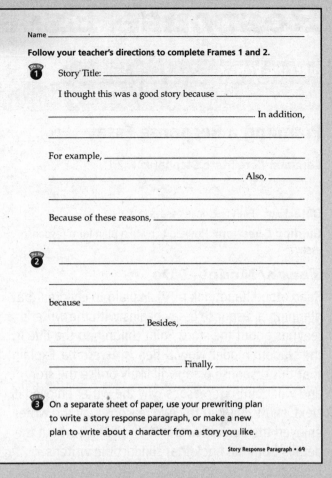

Topic Sentence
States the writer's opinion

Details and Examples
Support the writer's opinion

Linking Words
Connect ideas and organize the paragraph

Clear Ending
States the writer's opinion again

The dog in <u>The Dog That Dug for Dinosaurs</u> by Shirley Raye Redmond is a very smart animal. **For example**, the dog helps to find dinosaur bones. Tray sniffs and scratches the ground to show where the bones are. **Also**, Tray knows how to guard the bones. He growls to keep people away from them. **Sometimes**, Tray seems to answer his owner's questions by wagging his tail. In the story, Mr. Buckland calls Tray an intelligent dog. That means he really is a very smart dog.

Other Words that Link Ideas
Besides
In addition
Next
Finally
Because

Name _____

Follow your teacher's directions to complete Frames 1 and 2.

1 Story Title: _____

I thought this was a good story because _____
_____ In addition,
_____
For example, _____
_____ Also, _____

Because of these reasons, _____

2 _____
_____
because _____
_____ Besides, _____
_____
_____ Finally, _____
_____

3 On a separate sheet of paper, use your prewriting plan to write a story response paragraph, or make a new plan to write about a character from a story you like.

Corrective Feedback

IF . . . children struggle with topic sentences and concluding statements,

THEN . . . remind them that the topic sentence and concluding statement share the same idea. Encourage children to rewrite their topic sentence in a number of ways and to choose a concluding statement from among them. Suggest that they begin their concluding statements with a sentence beginner such as *I think that....*

Focus Trait: Ideas

Remind children that story response paragraphs can address any part of a story, such as the characters, the setting, or the plot. To generate ideas, children can begin with what they liked about a story. On the board, write:

What I like: _____

Two reasons why I like that:

1)

2)

Two examples from the story that show what I like:

1)

2)

Encourage children to use and modify this outline to generate ideas for writing their response paragraphs.

Response Essay: Prewriting

Minilesson 57

Planning a Response Essay

Common Core State Standard: W.2.1

Objective: Plan response essays.

Guiding Question: How do I create a plan for a response essay?

Teach/Model—I Do

Read aloud handbook p. 70. Explain to children that planning a response essay begins with the writer's feelings about the story. Point children to the title in the student model: Now & Ben *Is Awesome*. Explain that this response essay will likely praise the story and will point out reasons why the writer enjoyed it. Next, show children the two reasons why the writer enjoyed the book (Reason #1 and #2). Point out the details from the book that support the writer's feelings.

Guided Practice—We Do

With children's help, write on the board a two-column chart like the one in the student model. Together, fill in the chart. Begin by choosing a familiar story that they enjoyed. Ask them to identify two reasons why they liked the story. Then, ask them for details from the story that support their opinions.

Practice/Apply—You Do

COLLABORATIVE Have partners choose a story they have read and enjoyed. Ask them to complete a chart like the one in the We Do section, with two reasons why they enjoyed the story.

INDEPENDENT Have children make a plan for a response essay about their reaction to a story or a character in it. Ask them to include two or more reasons that support their opinion and to provide details that explain each reason.

Conference/Evaluate

Circulate as children write and help them formulate responses to the stories they chose. Remind them to include supporting reasons and details.

Minilesson 58

Including Examples from the Text

Common Core State Standard: W.2.1

Objective: Include examples from a text.

Guiding Question: How do I include examples from a text in my response essay?

Teach/Model—I Do

Review handbook p. 70. Remind children that response essays tell readers what the writer thought of a story or part of a story. Explain that the way a writer supports an opinion of the story is by showing examples from the story. When writers include the exact words from a story, the words appear inside quotation marks. On the board, write as an example, *The Haktaks live in a "humble little house."*

Guided Practice—We Do

 Direct children to Activity 1 on handbook p. 71. For Part A, help children list three books they have recently read. Then, guide them to choose one book and complete Part B, listing reasons, facts, and details about the book they chose. Remind children that if their examples are exact words from the story, they must use quotation marks.

Practice/Apply—You Do

 COLLABORATIVE Direct children to Activity 2. Ask them to work in groups to choose a story they like and to fill in a column chart. Remind them to support their reasons with examples from the text.

 INDEPENDENT Have children read the directions. Tell them to use their prewriting plan from Lesson 29 or to brainstorm new ideas using Graphic Organizer 7.

Conference/Evaluate

During the writing process, circulate and offer encouragement and help as needed. Evaluate using the rubric on p. 104.

 Digital
• eBook
• WriteSmart
• Interactive Lessons

Response Essay

A **response essay** tells about a book you have read. It describes your feelings and thoughts about the book.

Parts of a Response Essay

- A first sentence that tells the title of the reading and your opinion of it
- Information about what you have read
- Details and reasons that support your opinion
- A closing sentence that sums up your opinion

Brainstorming List
- Now & Ben
- Two of Everything
- The Dog That Dug for Dinosaurs
- The Mysterious Tadpole

Title: Now & Ben Is Awesome

Reason #1: Ben Franklin invented some great things.	Reason #2: Ben Franklin changed our world.
Funny chairs	Electricity
A clock with a second hand	Libraries and hospitals
The lightning rod	Post offices
	Fire departments

Name _____

Follow your teacher's directions to complete this page.

1 a. Three Books I Have Read

_____

_____

_____

b. Title: _____

Reason #1: _____	Reason #2: _____

2 On a separate sheet of paper, choose another book as the topic of a response essay. Then fill in a Column Chart with reasons and details that support your opinion.

3 On another sheet of paper, plan a response essay, or use what you have learned to improve another plan.

 ## Corrective Feedback

IF . . . children struggle to find examples from the text,

THEN . . . suggest that they place a bookmarker or sticky-note in the text near the parts that relate to their response essay. Encourage children to examine those parts to find words and phrases that serve as examples to support their responses.

 ## Focus Trait: Ideas

Explain to children that asking questions is a helpful way to find ideas to write about. On the board, write the following questions that might lead to a response.

What did I like about the story?

What would I like to change about the story?

Which character did I relate to or understand the best?

Why was the setting an important part of the story?

What lesson did the story try to teach?

Encourage children to ask these and other questions as they generate ideas for a response essay.

Grade 2 • **71**

Response Essay

Minilesson 59

Drafting a Response Essay

Common Core State Standards: W.2.1, W.2.5

Objective: Write a response essay that includes details.

Guiding Question: How can I respond to a story by supporting my opinion with reasons and details?

Teach/Model—I Do

Read aloud handbook p. 72. Point out the opinion, the details that support it, and the closing. Discuss how the boldfaced words help express opinions. Review the list of opinion words in the box.

Guided Practice—We Do

 Have children turn to handbook p. 73. Help them write an opening sentence for the frame that includes the title of a story, such as *I think everyone should read "Two of Everything."* Elicit reasons for the opinion and choose one to complete the second sentence. Help children select other details from the story that support the opinion. Add a closing. Have children write in their books as you write on the board.

Practice/Apply—You Do

 COLLABORATIVE For Activity 2, have small groups work together to choose a different story for a response. Tell them to write an opening sentence that includes the title of the story. Then have them write an opinion, details that support the opinion, and a closing.

 INDEPENDENT Have children read the directions. Tell them to use their prewriting plan from Lesson 30 or to brainstorm new ideas, using Graphic Organizer 1.

Conference/Evaluate

During the writing process, circulate and offer encouragement and help as needed. Evaluate using the rubric on p. 104.

Minilesson 60

Revising a Response Essay

Common Core State Standards: W.2.1, W.2.5

Objective: Revise a response essay.

Guiding Question: How can I make my response essay better?

Teach/Model—I Do

Point out the boldfaced words on handbook p. 72. Explain that *I think*, *best*, and *I feel* are opinion words. These words tell how the writer feels about *Now & Ben*. Guide children to understand that using opinion words helps convey how a writer feels about a selection. Explain that one way to revise a response essay is to add opinion words.

Guided Practice—We Do

Write the following sentences on the board: *I think Monsters on Main Street is a terrible book. I guessed the ending right away. It is the worst mystery I have ever read. Everyone should skip this story.* Work with children to identify opinion words *(I think, terrible, worst).* Point out that these words help readers understand how the writer feels about the mystery *Monsters on Main Street*. Guide children to add more opinion words to their drafts on p. 73.

Practice/Apply—You Do

COLLABORATIVE Have partners find and underline opinion words in their Activity 2 drafts. Then have them suggest places where opinion words could be added to make the writer's thoughts and feelings clearer to readers.

INDEPENDENT Have children find and underline opinion words in their Activity 3 drafts, adding opinion words where needed. Guide them to check that they have used strong reasons and details to support their opinion.

Conference/Evaluate

Have children review their revised drafts to make sure their response essays clearly state how they feel about a selection they have read.

- eBook
- WriteSmart
- Interactive Lessons

Response Essay

A **response essay** tells about a selection you have read. It also tells your thoughts and feelings.

Parts of a Response Essay

- An opening that gives the selection's title and your opinion
- Information about what you read
- Reasons and details to support your opinion
- Linking words that connect opinions to reasons
- A closing to sum up your opinion

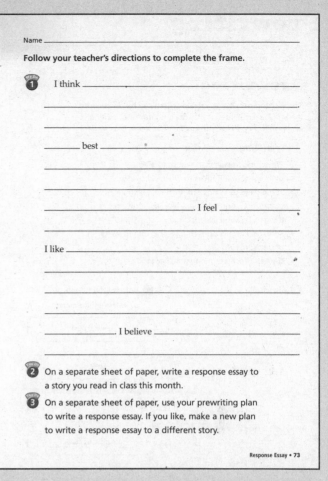

Opening
States title and your opinion

Reasons
Details that tell about the book and your opinion

Closing
Restates your opinion

I think *Now & Ben* is a very good book. I learned that Ben Franklin invented many things. Some of his **best** inventions were funny chairs and a clock with a second hand. He helped us use electricity, and he invented the lightning rod.

We should thank Ben for our libraries and hospitals, too. He also started post offices and fire departments. **I feel** everyone should read *Now & Ben* because Ben Franklin changed our world.

Opinion Words
I think
I feel
I like
I believe
Good
Wonderful
Best
Worst

Name _____

Follow your teacher's directions to complete the frame.

1 I think _____

_____

_____

_____ best _____

_____

_____

_____ I feel _____

_____

I like _____

_____

_____

_____ I believe _____

_____

2 On a separate sheet of paper, write a response essay to a story you read in class this month.

3 On a separate sheet of paper, use your prewriting plan to write a response essay. If you like, make a new plan to write a response essay to a different story.

Corrective Feedback

IF . . . children have difficulty writing their responses,

THEN . . . remind them to start by stating their opinion. Next, help them skim through the story to find details that support their opinion. Use the Opinion Words box on handbook p. 72 to review the different opinion words they can use.

Connect Focus: Word Choice

Write the following statements on the board and read them aloud.

If you mix red and blue together, you get purple.
I like the color purple.
Purple is the best color of all.

Remind children that they often have to read carefully to decide whether a statement is a fact or an opinion. The first sentence can be proved, so it is a fact. The second sentence starts with *I like*, which clearly shows it is an opinion. Ask children about the third sentence. Although it may sound like a fact, it is an opinion because it can't be proved. Write the following on the board and work with children to identify each as a fact or an opinion.

Summer is the best season of the year. (o)
Most schools close during the summer. (f)
I love summer vacation. (o)

Prewriting

Prewriting

The **writing process** is a strategy that can help you write. It has five stages: prewriting, drafting, revising, editing, and publishing. **Prewriting** is the first stage.

Prewriting

- Prewriting means planning before you write. Plan by brainstorming ideas to write about.
- Some ways to brainstorm include making lists, clustering, using what you already know, or looking through your journal.
- After you brainstorm, choose one idea to write about. Circle it.
- Gather information on your chosen idea, or topic.

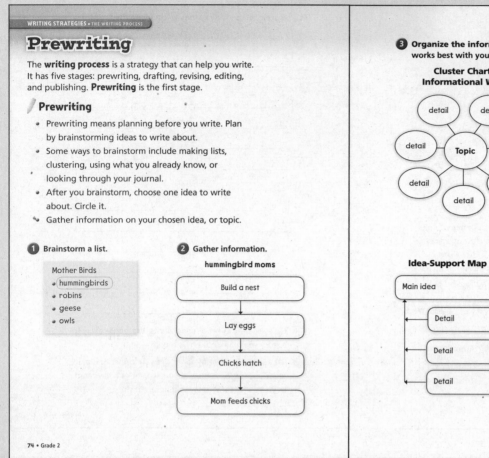

1 Brainstorm a list.

Mother Birds
- hummingbirds
- robins
- geese
- owls

2 Gather information.

hummingbird moms

Build a nest
↓
Lay eggs
↓
Chicks hatch
↓
Mom feeds chicks

3 **Organize the information.** Choose the Graphic Organizer that works best with your **TAP**. Here are some examples:

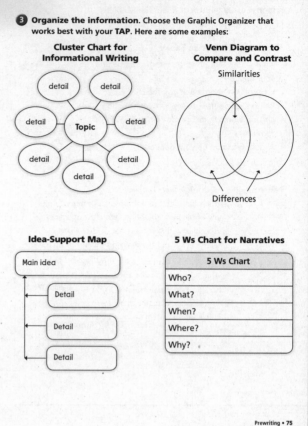

Cluster Chart for Informational Writing

detail detail
detail **Topic** detail
detail detail
detail

Venn Diagram to Compare and Contrast

Similarities

Differences

Idea-Support Map

Main idea
Detail
Detail
Detail

5 Ws Chart for Narratives

5 Ws Chart
Who?
What?
When?
Where?
Why?

Minilesson 61

Introducing Prewriting

Common Core State Standards: W.2.1, W.2.2, W.2.3

Objective: Understand how to use the Prewriting handbook pages.

Guiding Question: How do I use these pages to help me plan a written work?

Teach/Model

With children, read p. 74. Explain that the example on this page shows how brainstorming a list of topics helps writers choose a topic and organize information.

Practice/Apply

Read the graphic organizer on p. 74. Explain that each detail in the organizer relates to the main topic at the top. Ask children to describe how the information is arranged in the organizer (time order).

74 • Writing for Common Core

Minilesson 62

Using Graphic Organizers

Common Core State Standards: W.2.1, W.2.2, W.2.3

Objective: Understand how to use a graphic organizer.

Guiding Question: How can I use a graphic organizer to develop a prewriting plan?

Teach/Model

Examine the graphic organizers on p. 75. Explain that each organizer shows information differently. Point out the uses and strengths of each organizer. (Example: *A cluster chart helps you brainstorm details, while an idea-support map helps you put them in order.*)

Practice/Apply

Have children choose a graphic organizer that works best with their TAP. Ask children to fill in the organizer using information they know and understand.

Drafting

Drafting

Drafting means writing out your ideas. It is the second stage in the writing process. It is done after prewriting.

Drafting

- Use your prewriting ideas to help you draft.
- When you draft, turn your ideas into sentences.
- Don't worry about mistakes. You can make changes later.
- Begin with a topic sentence that tells what you are writing about. Then add details and a closing.

hummingbird moms

Build a nest → Lay eggs → Chicks hatch → Mom feeds chicks

Draft

Hummingbird mothers do a lot to help bring their babies into the world. First, a hummingbird builds a nest. Next, she lays eggs. Soon, the chicks hatch from the eggs. The baby hummingbirds are hungry! The mother hummingbird brings food for them. She helps them until they grow up.

Another Example

lightning — thunder — **Topic** rainstorms — beats against windows — puddles

Draft

Rainstorms can be very exciting. Lightning makes huge flashes in the sky. Scary thunder can make you hide under the bed. Sometimes the rain beats hard against my windows and even makes them shake. The next day there are lots of puddles. If you want to see the sky put on a big show, you will like watching a rainstorm!

WRITING STRATEGY

Minilesson 63

Introducing Drafting

Common Core State Standards: W.2.1, W.2.2, W.2.3

Objective: Understand how to use the Drafting handbook pages.

Guiding Question: How do I use these pages to help me start writing?

Teach/Model

Have children read p. 76. Point out that the graphic organizer uses time order to organize an informational paragraph.

Practice/Apply

Have children compare the information in the organizer with that in the paragraph. Discuss the importance of following the organizer while adding related information as they draft.

Minilesson 64

Going from Organizer to Draft

Common Core State Standards: W.2.1, W.2.2, W.2.3

Objective: Understand how to use a graphic organizer.

Guiding Question: How can I use my graphic organizer to draft an informational paragraph?

Teach/Model

Have children read p. 77. Explain that webs group together information related to a topic. Show children that writers can add related information to the organizer until they have enough material to draft. Model the process of putting information from the web into a paragraph.

Practice/Apply

Have children fill out a graphic organizer about another kind of weather, and then have them use it to write a paragraph.

Revising

Revising

Revising is the third stage of the writing process. When you revise, you change any parts that seem unclear or incomplete.

Revising

- Reread your draft to see if your ideas are clear.
- Add details that make your draft more interesting.
- Take out words that do not go with your topic.

Ways to Revise

- Use editor's marks to add, take out, or change words in your draft.
- Add sentences to show more detail.

Editor's Marks
∧ Add.
⟍⟋ Take out.
‾∧ Change.

> First, a hummingbird builds a nest. She uses small sticks and dandelion fuzz.
> ∧

- Combine sentences to cut words you don't need.

> The mother builds a small nest. She builds it out of small sticks and dandelion fuzz.

> two white
> Next, she lays eggs. Soon, the chicks hatch from the eggs.
> ∧

- Move information so that it is in an order that makes sense.

> ∧The mother hummingbird brings food for them. The babies are hungry!

Here's how a revised draft might look:

> Hummingbird mothers do a lot to help bring their babies into the world. First, a hummingbird
> out of small sticks and dandelion fuzz.
> builds a nest. Next, she lays eggs. Soon, the chicks
> two white
> hatch from the eggs. The mother hummingbird brings food for them. The baby hummingbirds are hungry!
> She helps them until they grow up.

WRITING STRATEGY

Minilesson 65

Introducing Revising

Common Core State Standard: W.2.5

Objective: Understand how to use the Revising handbook pages.

Guiding Question: How do I use these pages to revise my draft?

Teach/Model

Have children read pp. 78–79. Explain that revising can mean adding or taking out material to improve a draft. Point out the changes the writer made in the student models.

Practice/Apply

On the board, write the sentence *My day starts with breakfast and the bus.* Ask children to use editor's marks to improve the sentence.

Minilesson 66

Revising a Draft

Common Core State Standard: W.2.5

Objective: Understand how to revise a draft.

Guiding Question: What revision methods can I use to improve my draft?

Teach/Model

Review pp. 78 and 79. Remind children that revising requires writers to mark up their drafts using editor's marks. Explain that revising helps to create a clean, finished work.

Practice/Apply

Ask children to revise their drafts using the editor's marks on p. 78. Suggest that children share their work with a partner to check for clarity and mistakes.

Editing and Publishing

Editing

Editing is the fourth stage of the writing process. When you edit, you proofread your draft for mistakes. Then you correct any that you find.

Editing

- Proofread your draft and look for mistakes.
- Use editing marks to help you fix your writing.
- Check for complete sentences.
- Check for capital letters.
- Check for commas and end punctuation.
- Check for spelling and grammar errors.
- Use verbs and adjectives correctly.

Editor's Marks

∧ Add.

⤴ Take out.

Ⱥ Change.

Edited Draft

The mother builds a small nest out of tiny sticks and spider
webs. She fills the nest with ~~dandelion~~ dandelion fluff and cattail fuzz.
The nest is warm and ~~cozy~~ cozy. Then she lays two white eggs.
The the eggs are the size of peas.

Publishing

Publishing means sharing your writing. It is the last stage of the writing process. In this stage, you make a clean, final draft of your writing.

Publishing

- Write or type your final draft neatly, with margins and paragraph indents.
- Put your name on your work.
- Think of ways to share your writing, such as making it into a book, reading it aloud, or adding pictures.
- You can use a computer to choose pictures, charts, audio, or video to go with your writing.

Hummingbird Mothers
by Alice Montgomery

Hummingbird mothers do a lot to help bring their babies into the world. First, a hummingbird builds a nest out of small sticks and dandelion fuzz. Next, she lays two white eggs. Soon, the chicks hatch from the eggs. The baby hummingbirds are hungry! The mother hummingbird brings food for them. She helps them until they grow up.

Minilesson 67

Introducing Editing

Common Core State Standard: W.2.5

Objective: Understand how to use editor's marks to check for correct spelling and grammar.

Guiding Question: How do I use editor's marks to correct my draft?

Teach/Model

Have children read p. 80. Explain that once a writer finishes a draft, she must correct any remaining spelling and grammar errors.

Practice/Apply

Ask children to use the editor's marks to correct mistakes in their drafts. Remind them to consider all of the types of errors listed on p. 80.

Minilesson 68

Preparing to Publish

Common Core State Standard: W.2.6

Objective: Understand how to prepare a work for publication.

Guiding Question: How can I prepare my final draft for publishing?

Teach/Model

With children, read p. 81. Explain to children that preparing a work for publishing means getting it ready to share with others as a finished product. Discuss with children the way in which their final drafts will be published.

Practice/Apply

Ask children to write their final drafts using indentation, margins, and neat handwriting. Children may add images or charts to enhance their work.

Ideas

WRITING STRATEGIES • WRITING TRAITS

Ideas

There are six traits to follow for good writing. The traits are ideas, organization, voice, word choice, sentence fluency, and conventions. **Ideas** are what you write about.

Ideas

- Can come from what you know or what you learn
- Are supported by interesting details
- Can come from brainstorming or making lists

Make a List of Topics

Think of as many ideas as you can and make a list. Circle the ideas you like the most.

People	Places	Things
friends	home	books
family	school	swing set
mom	library	skateboard
teacher	Florida	school bus
doctor	science museum	board game

Sample Writing Idea: Friends

The word <u>friends</u> makes me think of Jodi and Lisa. I could write a story about the time we took a field trip to the science museum.

Narrative Writing

Write down ideas about people and events.
Good graphic organizers to use for ideas: story map, flow chart

Beginning: Joe wants to be a vet.

Middle: He visits his vet to see what she does.

End: He wants to go to vet school.

Informative Writing

Make a list of details and questions about a topic.
Good graphic organizers to use for ideas: web, idea-support map

Ideas for a Report About Pandas

What kind of animal are pandas?

Where do pandas live?

How do pandas raise their young?

What do pandas eat?

WRITING STRATEGY

Minilesson 69

Introducing Ideas

Common Core State Standards: W.2.1, W.2.2, W.2.3

Objective: Understand how listing and brainstorming can inspire ideas.

Guiding Question: How do I discover ideas for writing?

Teach/Model

Have children read p. 82. Point out how the circled words in the chart inspired the writing idea shown.

Practice/Apply

Ask children to create a chart like the student model using the headings *People, Activities,* and *Events.* Have children circle two ideas that inspire a potential narrative.

Minilesson 70

Brainstorming Ideas

Common Core State Standards: W.2.1, W.2.2, W.2.3

Objective: Understand how ideas for writing can come from graphic organizers.

Guiding Question: How can I use graphic organizers to think of ideas?

Teach/Model

With children, read pp. 82–83. Explain that the graphic organizer they use to think of ideas depends on the writing form.

Practice/Apply

Ask children to choose a graphic organizer for the topic *My Favorite Weekend Activity.* Have them fill in the graphic organizer and choose an idea for writing based on the details they generate.

Organization

Organization

Organization is the order in which you put your words and ideas. Different kinds of writing need different kinds of organization.

- Ideas can be in time order or in another order that makes sense.
- Narrative writing has a beginning, middle, and end.
- Informative and persuasive writing has an introduction, body, and conclusion.

Narrative Writing

- A beginning that gets readers interested
- A middle that describes at least one event
- An ending that tells how the event wrapped up

Beginning	Jodi's mom took us to the zoo. Jodi did not want to go. She was afraid of ostriches. She said they were tall and ugly. Maybe one would bite her. I thought ostriches were weird-looking but cool. I really wanted to see one. We went to a
Middle	bird exhibit and saw an ostrich behind a fence. He seemed very friendly. He had a long neck and long legs and a big body with lots of feathers. The ostrich looked at us and ran away. Jodi
End	laughed. She is not afraid of ostriches anymore.

Information Writing

- An introduction that states the main idea
- A body with supporting details that tell about the main idea
- A closing statement that ties ideas together

Introduction	Ostriches are unusual birds. For one thing, they can't fly. Instead, they can run very fast. Their long legs help them run up to 40 miles per
Body	hour. They are also the biggest kind of bird in the world. They lay huge eggs, too. They look strange, with long necks and small heads.
Conclusion	Ostriches are different from most birds.

Persuasive Writing

- A topic sentence that states your opinion
- Reasons and examples of why you feel that way
- An ending that tries to make your readers agree with you

Opinion	Ostriches are the best kinds of birds. First, they are big! Second, they can run really fast. They have special claws on their feet that look like hooves. Those help move their feet. It is
Reasons	okay that they can't fly because they can still move quickly. They also can hear and see very well. Ostriches are different from other kinds of
Ending	birds. That makes them more interesting.

WRITING STRATEGY

Minilesson 71

Introducing Organization

Common Core State Standards: W.2.3

Objective: Understand how paragraphs are organized.

Guiding Question: How do I organize a paragraph?

Teach/Model

Have children read p. 84. Explain that paragraph organization helps readers make sense of what they read. Read the student model, pointing out that, in a narrative, the events happen in time order.

Practice/Apply

Ask children to write a brief narrative that begins with the sentence *The little boat tossed and turned on the stormy waves.* Have them end their narratives with *The little boat made it safely to shore.* Ask children to organize the events in the middle of the narrative.

Minilesson 72

Organizing Informational and Persuasive Writing

Common Core State Standards: W.2.1, W.2.2

Objective: Understand how to organize informational and persuasive writing.

Guiding Question: How do I organize informational and persuasive writing?

Teach/Model

With children, read pp. 84–85. Point out the topic and concluding sentences in each model. Explain that different kinds of writing require different kinds of organization. Review the bulleted points.

Practice/Apply

Ask children to write a topic sentence and a concluding sentence for an informational paragraph about making an inventive, new sandwich.

Voice and Word Choice

Voice

Voice shows what a writer is like.

Voice

- You have your own style and voice.
- Use your voice to speak to your readers.
- Share how you think and feel.
- Whenever you write, keep your purpose in mind.
- Match your voice with your purpose. Are you writing to describe, tell a story, explain, or persuade?

Informative Voice
Use specific details to explain your topic. Help your reader to understand information or follow steps.

> First, spread glue on your drawing in the spots where you want the glitter to go. Next, sprinkle the glitter on the glue. Let it dry for a minute. Then shake the extra glitter off. Finally, let your picture dry.

Persuasive Voice
Use good reasons so that the reader will agree with you.

> It is always good to wear a hat on a cold day. You lose a lot of heat from the top of your head. A hat helps to keep your whole body warm.

Word Choice

The words you choose help create a picture for your reader.

Word Choice

- Choose words that best tell your ideas.
- Revise your work to change dull, unclear words. Replace them with exact words.

Exact Words
- Clearly describe what characters are thinking and feeling
- Clearly describe what is happening
- Make people, places, and things easy for readers to see

> **Not Exact**
>
> Lina went to Jake's party. She was happy to go. She had a gift. She hoped Jake liked it.

> **Exact**
>
> Lina skipped down the street on the way to Jake's birthday party. She was so excited to go. She brought a gift wrapped in colorful paper. She was sure Jake would like it, since he had been talking about it for weeks!

WRITING STRATEGY

Minilesson 73

Introducing Voice

Common Core State Standard: L.2.3

Objective: Understand how to use voice in writing.

Guiding Question: How do I use voice to make my writing unique?

Teach/Model

Have children read p. 86. Explain that voice in writing is as unique as the writer and that a writer's voice changes to match the purpose of the writing.

Practice/Apply

With the children, read both student models. Point out the time-order words, such as *next* and *finally*, that create an informative voice. Ask children to find words that create a persuasive voice, such as *good*, *you*, and *a lot*, in the second model.

Minilesson 74

Introducing Word Choice

Common Core State Standard: W.2.3

Objective: Understand how word choice conveys details.

Guiding Question: How do I use word choice to convey details in my writing?

Teach/Model

With children, read p. 87. Explain that details paint pictures in the reader's minds. Word choice is what helps readers paint those pictures.

Practice/Apply

Discuss the differences between the two student models. Have children identify vivid words in the second model—such as *skipped, excited,* and *colorful*—that paint pictures for the reader.

Sentence Fluency

Sentence Fluency

Sentence fluency means a writer's sentences flow together smoothly. Sentence fluency makes your writing clearer and easier to read.

Sentence Fluency

- Make some sentences short or long.
- Connect ideas from sentence to sentence.
- Use different sentence beginnings.

Make some sentences short or long.

Sentences all the same length	Combine into longer, smoother ones
I like to ride my bike. I like to ride it downhill. It is fast.	I like to ride my bike. It is fun to ride it downhill fast.
The house was old. It was made of stone. It was made of wood, too.	The old house was made of stone and wood.

Connect ideas from sentence to sentence.

Choppy sentences	Use time-order words
I saw the rabbit in the garden. I saw the rabbit in the garden today.	Yesterday, I saw the rabbit in the garden. I saw him again today.

Use different sentence beginnings.

Too many sentences with the same beginning	Variety of sentence beginnings
Florida is the best state. Florida is not like other states. Florida is warm and sunny. It is near the ocean. You can enjoy the beach.	Florida is the best state. Unlike other states, it is warm and sunny. Since Florida is near the ocean, you can enjoy the beach.

Here is an example of how to fix sentences to make them more fluent in a paragraph.

Choppy First Draft	Revised Draft
Birds live in different kinds of nests. Birds lay eggs in the nests. Birds take care of their babies in the nests. Nests come in many sizes and shapes. Nests are made from leaves or twigs.	Birds live in different kinds of nests. They build their nests in many sizes and shapes. Most make their nests from twigs or leaves. The nests may look different, but all birds lay eggs in their nests and take care of their babies there, too.

WRITING STRATEGY

Minilesson 75

Introducing Sentence Fluency

Common Core State Standard: W.2.5

Objective: Understand how to write fluent sentences.

Guiding Question: How do I write fluent sentences that are easy to read?

Teach/Model

With children, read p. 88. Point out the changes the writer made in each student model to improve sentence fluency. Discuss how the sentences were improved.

Practice/Apply

Ask children to point out the key words that were kept or added to create sentence fluency. Discuss with children whether the meaning of the sentences was changed when the sentences were revised.

Minilesson 76

Creating Fluency in Paragraphs

Common Core State Standard: W.2.5

Objective: Understand how sentence fluency improves paragraphs.

Guiding Question: How do I use sentence fluency to make paragraphs flow?

Teach/Model

With children, read the student models on p. 89. Explain that, along with sentence length and sentence beginnings, sentence order can be changed for fluency.

Practice/Apply

Ask children to discuss the differences between the choppy paragraph and the revised draft. Point out that sentences were combined, pronouns were added, and sentences were reordered to add fluency.

Conventions

Conventions

Conventions are rules for grammar, spelling, punctuation, and capitalization. When you edit your writing, you check for conventions.

Conventions

- Follow grammar and punctuation rules.
- Check your spelling.
- Check your capitalization.
- Edit and proofread your writing.

Editing Checklist
Use an editing checklist to review your writing.

____	My sentences are different lengths.
____	My sentences are complete.
____	I have used punctuation correctly.
____	My words are all spelled correctly.
____	I have used capitalization correctly.

Subjects and Predicates
A sentence should have both a subject and a predicate.

Wrong Way	Right Way
The roller coaster.	The roller coaster is my favorite ride.
Better than other rides.	I like it better than other rides.

Singular and Plural Nouns
Singular nouns are used for one person or thing. Plural nouns are used for more than one person or thing.

Wrong Way	Right Way
He wanted to make many friend.	He wanted to make many friends.
I put one ice cubes in my juice.	I put one ice cube in my juice.

Capitalization
Proper nouns should always be capitalized.

Wrong Way	Right Way
Next week, I am going to orlando with my brother ricardo.	Next week, I am going to Orlando with my brother Ricardo.

Correct use of commas in dates and places
Commas separate months and days from years. They are also used to separate cities or towns from states.

Wrong Way	Right Way
He was born on March, 31 2000 in Miami Florida.	He was born on March 31, 2000 in Miami, Florida.

WRITING STRATEGY

Minilesson 77

Introducing Conventions

Common Core State Standards: L.2.1, L.2.2

Objective: Understand grammar conventions.

Guiding Question: How do I use grammar conventions to improve my writing?

Teach/Model

With children, read pp. 90–91. Explain to children that grammar conventions make writing correct and easier to understand. Review the grammar conventions in the bulleted list on p. 91.

Practice/Apply

With children, read each Wrong Way and Right Way on p. 91. Ask children to identify what was added or changed in each Right Way to correct the writing.

Minilesson 78

Editing a Draft for Conventions

Common Core State Standards: W.2.5, L.2.1, L.2.2

Objective: Understand how to edit a draft for grammar conventions.

Guiding Question: How do I edit my draft for grammar conventions?

Teach/Model

Explain that good writers strive for grammatical correctness in everything they write. With children, review the examples on p. 91.

Practice/Apply

Ask children to edit their own drafts for grammar conventions using the Editing Checklist on p. 90. Encourage them to use the definitions and examples on p. 91 as they check their work.

Writing Workshop

Writing Workshop

In a writing workshop, you share your writing with others. You can help each other make your writing better.

Being Part of a Writing Workshop

- Listen carefully to your classmates' ideas.
- Make changes that make sense to you.
- Listen when others read their work.
- Tell what you like about their work.
- Give only helpful ideas.

The Beach

by Kristi Jones

> *Use sense words to tell us about the picnic.*

Last week I went to the beach with my family. First, we made sand castles. Then we had a picnic for lunch.

> *I really like this line! I can feel the scrunch.*

Later, we played on the beach. We threw a ball back and forth. My feet went scrunch on the sand.

> *We know you aren't really a shark, so you don't need this part!*

Finally, we went swimming. I pretended I was a shark. I wasn't really a shark, though. Then we went home.

Tips for Helping One Another

Sharing your writing with a partner can help you with the writing process. Here are some ways partners can help one another during the writing process.

Talk

- Partners can talk about topics and details. Talking can help you think of ideas.

Listen and Ask

- Partners can listen to or read a first draft. Partners ask questions and make suggestions to help revise the writing.

Check

- Partners can help check writing for conventions. They can help you find and fix mistakes.

Read

- Partners can read and enjoy a final copy. Presenting your writing so that it can be read is one way to publish.

WRITING STRATEGY

Minilesson 79

Introducing the Writing Workshop

Common Core State Standard: W.2.5

Objective: Understand rules for a writing workshop.

Guiding Question: How do I participate in a writing workshop?

Teach/Model

With children, read p. 92. Explain that a writing workshop works best if participants follow the workshop rules. Point out how the feedback in the left margin of the model is helpful and respectful.

Practice/Apply

Read children a series of possible responses to student work, such as *This ending is weird* and *Use time-order words.* Have children evaluate whether each response is constructive and rephrase those that are not.

Minilesson 80

Using Tips During a Writing Workshop

Common Core State Standard: W.2.5

Objective: Understand how to use a list of tips during a writing workshop.

Guiding Question: How do I use the list of tips to help my partner during a workshop?

Teach/Model

Review p. 93. Explain that a successful workshop depends on using the same set of tips, or guidelines for discussion.

Practice/Apply

Partner children and ask them to conduct a writing workshop using their current drafts. Have them follow the Tips for Helping One Another as they discuss each other's drafts.

Using the Internet

WRITING STRATEGIES • TECHNOLOGY

Using the Internet

Using the Internet is a great way to find information. You can search for websites to answer your questions or help with a report.

- A search engine will help you find websites about a topic.
- Many websites tell about an idea, person, place, or thing. If you are not sure whether a website you find is a good source, ask your teacher or parent.
- Write down your sources. Be sure to write the address of the website and the title.

✏ Parts of a Website

URL/Address Line

Title

Websites can link you to people and places around the world. They can help you learn more about a topic. For example, a zoo website might have interesting facts about tigers.

A website for a flower store might have information about roses.

These links can take you to pages with more information.

A website about outdoor fun might tell you things to do in the snow.

Websites can also show lists and photos.

WRITING STRATEGY

Minilesson 81

Introducing "Using the Internet"

Common Core State Standards: W.2.2, W.2.6

Objective: Understand how searching the Internet can help writers locate information.

Guiding Question: How do I search the Internet to find information for a report?

Teach/Model

Read p. 94. Explain that a search engine looks through the Internet for websites related to a topic that the user provides. Point out that the user must determine whether the site is useful and trustworthy.

Practice/Apply

Ask children what topic a search engine might have been given in order to find this site. Ask them what report topics might relate to information on this site.

Minilesson 82

Using the Internet to Locate Information

Common Core State Standards: W.2.2, W.2.6

Objective: Understand how Internet pages can provide writers with information.

Guiding Question: How do I use information from the Internet to write a report?

Teach/Model

With children, read p. 95. Point out that the Roses Roses! website might provide information about roses for a report on flowers.

Practice/Apply

Ask children what they might expect to read about under each link on the web page shown. If computers are available, have children use the Internet to locate information about another type of flower.

Writing for the Web

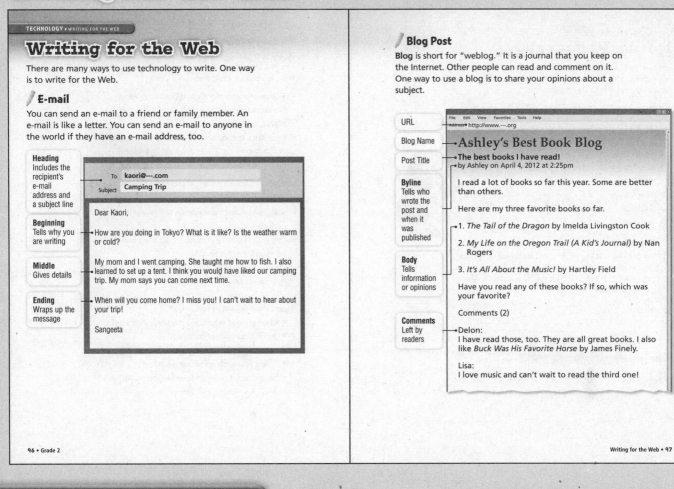

Writing for the Web

There are many ways to use technology to write. One way is to write for the Web.

E-mail

You can send an e-mail to a friend or family member. An e-mail is like a letter. You can send an e-mail to anyone in the world if they have an e-mail address, too.

Heading Includes the recipient's e-mail address and a subject line

To: kaori@---.com
Subject: Camping Trip

Beginning Tells why you are writing

Dear Kaori,

How are you doing in Tokyo? What is it like? Is the weather warm or cold?

Middle Gives details

My mom and I went camping. She taught me how to fish. I also learned to set up a tent. I think you would have liked our camping trip. My mom says you can come next time.

Ending Wraps up the message

When will you come home? I miss you! I can't wait to hear about your trip!

Sangeeta

Blog Post

Blog is short for "weblog." It is a journal that you keep on the Internet. Other people can read and comment on it. One way to use a blog is to share your opinions about a subject.

URL

Blog Name

Post Title

Byline Tells who wrote the post and when it was published

Body Tells information or opinions

Comments Left by readers

File Edit View Favorites Tools Help
Address http://www.---.org

Ashley's Best Book Blog

The best books I have read!
by Ashley on April 4, 2012 at 2:25pm

I read a lot of books so far this year. Some are better than others.

Here are my three favorite books so far.

1. *The Tail of the Dragon* by Imelda Livingston Cook
2. *My Life on the Oregon Trail (A Kid's Journal)* by Nan Rogers
3. *It's All About the Music!* by Hartley Field

Have you read any of these books? If so, which was your favorite?

Comments (2)

Delon:
I have read those, too. They are all great books. I also like *Buck Was His Favorite Horse* by James Finely.

Lisa:
I love music and can't wait to read the third one!

WRITING STRATEGY

Minilesson 83

Writing E-Mail

Common Core State Standard: W.2.6

Objective: Understand how to write an e-mail.

Guiding Question: How do I write an e-mail?

Teach/Model

Read p. 96. Point out the parts of an e-mail and how it is similar to a postal letter. Explain that e-mail, or electronic mail, uses the Internet to travel from one computer to another. Children can send an e-mail to anyone in the world and it will arrive in an instant.

Practice/Apply

Ask children to compose an e-mail to a friend, using the model as an example to guide them. If computers are unavailable, have children write their e-mails on paper.

Minilesson 84

Writing Blog Posts

Common Core State Standard: W.2.6

Objective: Understand how writers build Internet blogs.

Guiding Question: How do I present and discuss information using the Web?

Teach/Model

With children, read p. 97. Use the model to point out the parts of a blog and how it is similar to a journal entry written on paper. Explain that blogs are open for comments and discussion by anyone reading the blog.

Practice/Apply

Ask children to write a brief blog entry about a favorite book or activity. Then have two partners add their comments, modeled after the example on p. 97. This can be done on paper if computers are unavailable.

Doing Research

Doing Research

The best way to support your informative or persuasive writing is to use facts and details. The best way to find facts and details is to do research.

Where to Find Information for Research

- Books
- Encyclopedias and other reference books
- Magazines
- Newspapers
- Digital Audio, CDs, DVDs
- The Internet
- Television and Videos
- Interviews

Sources

Sources are the places you get your information. Some sources are more reliable than others. Be sure to ask your teacher, parent, or librarian if a source is reliable. Always remember to record your sources.

Source List

Book:	Hummingbirds by Diane Swanson
Magazine:	Birdwatcher's Digest
Newspaper:	"Best Places to See Birds in Florida" from Sunshine Times website

Finding Information in a Library

A library is organized to help you find information. The books in a library are divided into three main sections: Fiction, Nonfiction, and Reference Books.

- **Fiction** includes stories and chapter books.
- **Nonfiction** books have facts about real people, places, and things.
- **Reference** books include encyclopedias, atlases, and dictionaries. These are kept in a special section of the library.

In addition to books, other reference materials may be available in your library.

- **Magazines and Newspapers** are found in the periodicals area.
- **Computers** with a connection to the Internet may be found in your library.
- **Media**, such as DVDs and CDs, may also be found in your library.

> **Tips: What does a librarian do?**
> - chooses and organizes the library's books
> - helps you find information
> - knows where everything is in the library
> - helps you with computer searches
> - shows you books and stories you might like

WRITING STRATEGY

Minilesson 85

Doing Research

Common Core State Standard: W.2.7

Objective: Understand how to do research.

Guiding Question: How does source information help me to do research?

Teach/Model

With children, read p. 98. Explain that what writers use as source material depends on the subject they are researching. Discuss the kinds of information that can be found in each source (such as news articles, more in depth articles, and so on).

Practice/Apply

Have children determine the writer's research subject based on the Source List on p. 98. Discuss how the first and last sources narrow down the topic more than the magazine on the list.

Minilesson 86

Using the Library to Research

Common Core State Standard: W.2.7

Objective: Understand how libraries and librarians play a part in doing research.

Guiding Question: How do I use the library and librarians to do research?

Teach/Model

Read p. 99. Explain that librarians can help find sources within the various sections of the library. Review the list *What does a librarian do?*

Practice/Apply

Ask children to choose a research topic, such as a favorite activity. Then have them identify possible sources for the topic. Example: *Topic: skateboarding Sources: sports magazine, website, DVD*

Notetaking

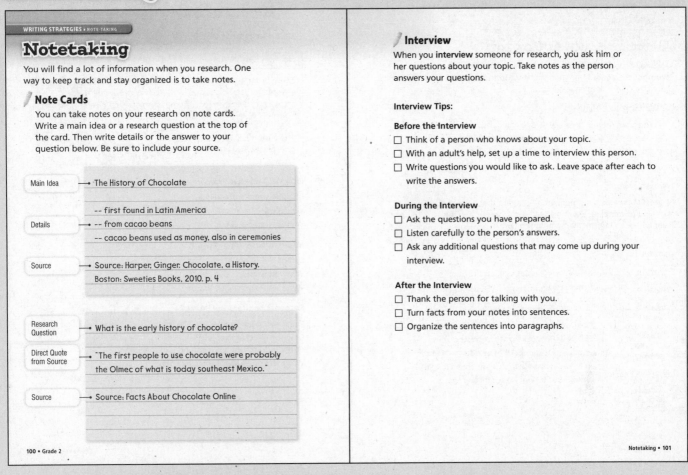

Notetaking

You will find a lot of information when you research. One way to keep track and stay organized is to take notes.

Note Cards

You can take notes on your research on note cards. Write a main idea or a research question at the top of the card. Then write details or the answer to your question below. Be sure to include your source.

Main Idea → The History of Chocolate

Details → -- first found in Latin America
-- from cacao beans
-- cacao beans used as money, also in ceremonies

Source → Source: Harper, Ginger. Chocolate, a History. Boston: Sweeties Books, 2010. p. 4

Research Question → What is the early history of chocolate?

Direct Quote from Source → "The first people to use chocolate were probably the Olmec of what is today southeast Mexico."

Source → Source: Facts About Chocolate Online

Interview

When you **interview** someone for research, you ask him or her questions about your topic. Take notes as the person answers your questions.

Interview Tips:

Before the Interview
- ☐ Think of a person who knows about your topic.
- ☐ With an adult's help, set up a time to interview this person.
- ☐ Write questions you would like to ask. Leave space after each to write the answers.

During the Interview
- ☐ Ask the questions you have prepared.
- ☐ Listen carefully to the person's answers.
- ☐ Ask any additional questions that may come up during your interview.

After the Interview
- ☐ Thank the person for talking with you.
- ☐ Turn facts from your notes into sentences.
- ☐ Organize the sentences into paragraphs.

WRITING STRATEGY

Minilesson 87

Introducing Notetaking

Common Core State Standard: W.2.2

Objective: Understand how to take notes.

Guiding Question: How do I take notes as part of the research process?

Teach/Model

With children, read p. 100. Point out the main idea (the history of chocolate) of the note cards. Explain that facts and quotations are useful information when writing a research paper.

Practice/Apply

Ask children to identify material on the note cards that might need more research, such as *cacao bean* or *the Olmec*. Have them write a research question about the unfamiliar material *(Where do cacao beans grow?)*.

Minilesson 88

Taking Notes During an Interview

Common Core State Standard: W.2.2

Objective: Understand how to take notes during an interview.

Guiding Question: How do I conduct an interview?

Teach/Model

Read p. 101. Explain that interviewing an expert can provide valuable information on a topic. Remind children that listening is an important part of an interview, as it will help them take the best notes.

Practice/Apply

Ask children to interview a partner about something they do well, such as a sport or a craft. Have children use the Interview Tips to prepare for and conduct the interview.

Writing to a Prompt

Writing to a Prompt

You may be writing to a prompt in class and on tests. A **prompt** asks a question. When you write to the prompt, answer all parts of the question.

✎ Writing to a Prompt

- Read the prompt carefully. Answer all parts.
- Give details and examples to explain your answer.
- Plan ahead. If the writing is timed, your teacher will tell you when to stop writing.

Written Prompts

A **written prompt** is a statement or question that asks you to complete a writing task. Here is an example of an **informative writing** prompt.

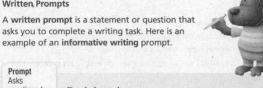

| Prompt
Asks questions for you to answer | → Read about the moon.
  What does it look like? How does it move?
  Write sentences about the moon. |
| Details
Give facts that answer the first part of the prompt | → The moon is round. It has light and dark spots. The dark spots are called craters. The |
| Details
Give facts that answer the next part of the prompt | → moon moves around Earth. The same side of the moon always faces Earth. The moon may always be round, but the way we see it changes. |

Here are some types of written prompts:

Fictional Narrative	Persuasive Writing
These prompts ask you to "tell a story."	These prompts ask you to "convince" or "persuade."
Informative Writing	**Response to Literature**
These prompts ask you to "tell or explain why."	These prompts ask you to answer questions about a piece you read.

Fictional Narrative Prompt:

Imagine you are an animal.

What type of animal would you be?

Write sentences about what you eat and how you live.

Informative Writing Prompt:

Saturn is a planet in our solar system.

What does Saturn look like?

Write sentences about Saturn.

Response to Literature Prompt:

Think about a character you like from a book you've read.

Describe the character and tell what you like about him or her.

Write sentences about this character.

WRITING STRATEGY

Minilesson 89

Introducing "Writing to a Prompt"

Common Core State Standard: W.2.2

Objective: Understand how a writing prompt works.
Guiding Question: How do I use a writing prompt to complete a writing task?

Teach/Model

Read p. 102. Point out that an informative prompt, like the one shown, asks for information or directions. Tell children that a writing prompt often has multiple parts that writers need to address.

Practice/Apply

Ask children to read the sample prompt. Then have them check the information in the paragraph against the prompt. Discuss whether the writer addressed all parts of the writing prompt.

Minilesson 90

Writing to a Prompt

Common Core State Standard: W.2.2

Objective: Understand how to write to different types of prompts.
Guiding Question: How do I write to a prompt?

Teach/Model

Read p. 103. Point out the differences between the four types of writing prompts. Explain that each type of writing prompt requires a different kind of written response.

Practice/Apply

Have children choose one prompt on p. 103 and write a brief response. Then have partners compare their writing to the prompt and its type to check for completion.

Checklists and Rubrics

Checklists and Rubrics

A **rubric** is a chart that helps you when you write and revise. Score 6 tells you what to aim for in your writing.

	• Focus • Support	• Organization
Score **6**	My writing is focused. It has facts or details.	My writing has a beginning and an ending. Ideas are in order.
Score **5**	My writing is mostly focused. It has facts or details.	My writing has a beginning and an ending. Most ideas are in order.
Score **4**	My writing is mostly focused. It has some facts or details.	My writing has a beginning and an ending. Some ideas are in order.
Score **3**	Some of my writing is focused. It has some facts or details.	My writing might have a beginning and an ending. Some ideas are in order.
Score **2**	My writing is not focused. It has few facts or details.	My writing might be missing a beginning or an ending. Few ideas are in order.
Score **1**	My writing is not focused. It has no facts or details.	My writing is missing a beginning or an ending. Few or no ideas are in order.

Circle a number in each row to rate your work. Then revise your writing to improve your score.

• Word Choice • Voice	• Conventions • Sentence Fluency
Ideas are connected with words. I use words that describe. My voice connects with the reader.	My writing has no errors in spelling, grammar, capitalization, or punctuation. Sentences have different lengths.
Most ideas are connected with words. I use some words that describe. My voice connects with the reader.	My writing has few errors in spelling, grammar, capitalization, or punctuation. Most sentences have different lengths.
Some ideas are connected with words. I use some words that describe. My voice may connect with the reader.	My writing has some errors in spelling, grammar, capitalization, or punctuation. Some sentences have different lengths.
Some ideas are connected with words. I use few words that describe. My voice may not connect with the reader.	My writing has some errors in spelling, grammar, capitalization, or punctuation. Few sentences have different lengths.
Few ideas are connected with words. I use few words that describe. My voice may not connect with the reader.	My writing has many errors in spelling, grammar, capitalization, or punctuation. Few sentences have different lengths.
Ideas are not connected with words. I use few words that describe. My voice does not connect with the reader.	My writing has many errors in spelling, grammar, capitalization, or punctuation. No sentences have different lengths. Sentences are incomplete.

WRITING STRATEGY

Minilesson 91

Introducing the Rubric

Common Core State Standard: W.2.5

Objective: Understand how a writing rubric works.

Guiding Question: How does a rubric help me write?

Teach/Model

Show children the rubric on pp. 104–105. Note the seven bulleted characteristics of writing at the top. Explain that a rubric can remind writers of the characteristics of good writing before they start to write.

Practice/Apply

Discuss the details required to score a 6. Discuss with children what it means when writing has focus, support, and voice.

Minilesson 92

Using a Rubric to Evaluate Writing

Common Core State Standard: W.2.5

Objective: Understand how to evaluate writing using a rubric.

Guiding Question: How do I use a rubric to evaluate my writing?

Teach/Model

Show children that rubrics allow writers to look at different aspects of their work, such as grammar and content. Explain to children that writing may score a 6 in one category but less in another.

Practice/Apply

Have children evaluate a piece of writing using the rubric on pp. 104–105. After evaluating, ask them to suggest changes that might improve the piece.

Sentences About a Picture/Paragraph

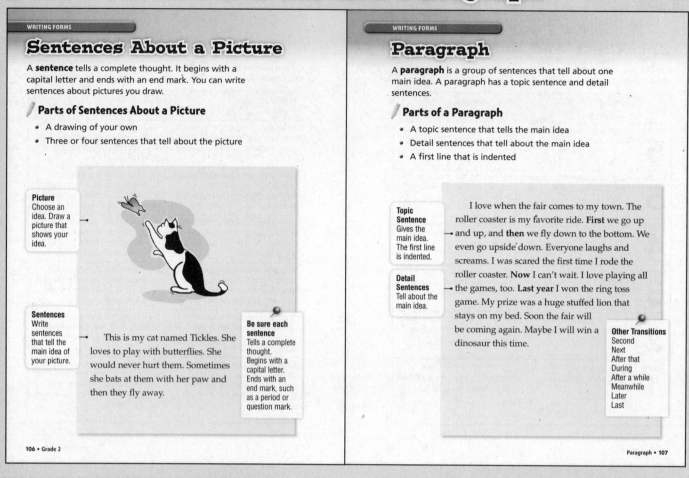

Sentences About a Picture

A **sentence** tells a complete thought. It begins with a capital letter and ends with an end mark. You can write sentences about pictures you draw.

Parts of Sentences About a Picture

- A drawing of your own
- Three or four sentences that tell about the picture

Picture
Choose an idea. Draw a picture that shows your idea.

Sentences
Write sentences that tell the main idea of your picture.

This is my cat named Tickles. She loves to play with butterflies. She would never hurt them. Sometimes she bats at them with her paw and then they fly away.

Be sure each sentence
Tells a complete thought. Begins with a capital letter. Ends with an end mark, such as a period or question mark.

Paragraph

A **paragraph** is a group of sentences that tell about one main idea. A paragraph has a topic sentence and detail sentences.

Parts of a Paragraph

- A topic sentence that tells the main idea
- Detail sentences that tell about the main idea
- A first line that is indented

Topic Sentence
Gives the main idea. The first line is indented.

Detail Sentences
Tell about the main idea.

I love when the fair comes to my town. The roller coaster is my favorite ride. **First** we go up and up, and **then** we fly down to the bottom. We even go upside down. Everyone laughs and screams. I was scared the first time I rode the roller coaster. **Now** I can't wait. I love playing all the games, too. **Last year** I won the ring toss game. My prize was a huge stuffed lion that stays on my bed. Soon the fair will be coming again. Maybe I will win a dinosaur this time.

Other Transitions
Second
Next
After that
During
After a while
Meanwhile
Later
Last

WRITING MODELS AND FORMS

Minilesson 93

Understanding Sentences About a Picture

Common Core State Standard: W.2.3

Objective: Understand how to use the information presented about sentences about a picture.

Guiding Question: How can I use these pages to help me write good sentences about a picture?

Teach/Model

Read the definition and bulleted points to children. Review the information in the boxes. Emphasize that when they write about a picture, they should use complete sentences.

Practice/Apply

Draw a picture on the board. Have children suggest sentences that tell the main idea of the picture.

Minilesson 94

Understanding Paragraphs

Common Core State Standard: W.2.2

Objective: Understand how to use the information presented about paragraphs.

Guiding Question: How can I use these pages to help me write a good paragraph?

Teach/Model

Read the definition and bulleted points to children. Read the model aloud with them. Add that a paragraph should also have a conclusion that ties the ideas together.

Practice/Apply

Discuss the model with children. Have them identify the main idea and supporting details in the model.

Descriptive Paragraph

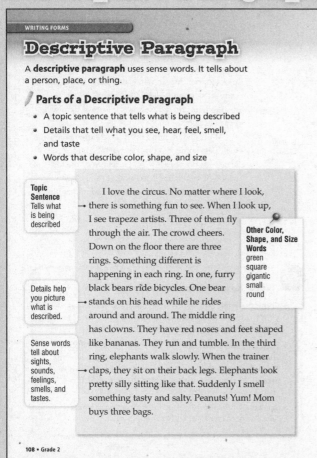

Descriptive Paragraph

A **descriptive paragraph** uses sense words. It tells about a person, place, or thing.

Parts of a Descriptive Paragraph

- A topic sentence that tells what is being described
- Details that tell what you see, hear, feel, smell, and taste
- Words that describe color, shape, and size

Topic Sentence
Tells what is being described

Details help you picture what is described.

Sense words tell about sights, sounds, feelings, smells, and tastes.

I love the circus. No matter where I look, there is something fun to see. When I look up, I see trapeze artists. Three of them fly through the air. The crowd cheers. Down on the floor there are three rings. Something different is happening in each ring. In one, furry black bears ride bicycles. One bear stands on his head while he rides around and around. The middle ring has clowns. They have red noses and feet shaped like bananas. They run and tumble. In the third ring, elephants walk slowly. When the trainer claps, they sit on their back legs. Elephants look pretty silly sitting like that. Suddenly I smell something tasty and salty. Peanuts! Yum! Mom buys three bags.

Other Color, Shape, and Size Words
green
square
gigantic
small
round

This topic sentence begins with an interesting description.

My dog Marlo is the best. His fur is soft and brown, but his paws are white. He looks like he's wearing socks. His ears are floppy. One ear looks longer than the other. Marlo's legs are pretty short, but he can run fast. He loves to play catch. You wouldn't believe how high he can jump, even though he's a little guy. Marlo plays hard, but he sleeps hard, too. Marlo will only sleep with me. Dad had to build special pet steps so Marlo could climb onto my bed. Once he's asleep, he doesn't move all night. The next morning, he's ready to run and play all over again. I don't know what I would do without Marlo. I have human friends, but Marlo is my very best friend of all.

Ending
Ties the paragraph together

Note how the authors of these descriptions:

- Introduced the topic at the beginning.
  I love the circus. No matter where I look, there is something fun to see.
  My dog Marlo is the best.

- Described many senses, not just sight.
  The crowd cheers.
  Suddenly I smell something tasty and salty.

WRITING MODELS AND FORMS

Minilesson 95

Understanding the Descriptive Paragraph

Common Core State Standard: W.2.2

Objective: Understand how to use the information presented about descriptive paragraphs.

Guiding Question: How can I use these pages to help me write a good descriptive paragraph?

Teach/Model

Read the definition and bulleted points to children. Tell children that a descriptive paragraph helps readers imagine what the writer is telling about. Review the box of sense words on p. 108.

Practice/Apply

Discuss the model with children. Ask them to find the sense words the author used to describe the circus.

Minilesson 96

Using Sense Words

Common Core State Standard: W.2.2

Objective: Use sense words to write a descriptive paragraph.

Guiding Question: How do I use sense words to write a descriptive paragraph?

Teach/Model

Tell children that sense words are words that describe the way a thing looks, sounds, feels, smells, or tastes. Give them examples of each.

Practice/Apply

Show children pictures of various objects, such as an apple, a guitar, or a flower. Have them write a sentence about each using sense words. Ask for volunteers to share their work with the class.

Summary

Summary

A **summary** uses your own words to tell the main ideas or events in a story.

Parts of a Summary

- A beginning that tells the title of the story
- A short retelling of the plot, characters, and setting in your own words
- The most important details or events from the story or article
- Events told in the order in which they happen

Beginning
Gives the name of the story and tells what it is about

Middle
Gives details that tell about the characters, plot, and setting

Details tell the most important events in the order they happen

Summary of *Teacher's Pets*

Teacher's Pets is a story by Dayle Ann Dodds. It is a story about a class and their pets.

In the story, Miss Fry lets her students bring their pets to class. First, Winston brings his pet rooster, Red. He leaves Red behind, so Miss Fry feeds him. The next day, Winston asks if he can leave Red in the classroom for a while. Miss Fry says yes.

Next, Patrick brings his pet tarantula and leaves him in the classroom, too. Then Roger brings in his cricket, Moe. Then all the students bring their pets.

Other Transitions
First
Next
After that
During
After a while
Meanwhile
Later
Last

Miss Fry takes care of the pets after the children leave. She talks to the pets and they do tricks for her. After a while, the whole school can hear the very noisy pets! On Parents' Night, all the mothers and fathers think it is great that Miss Fry likes pets so much.

At the end of the year, all the children take their pets home. But one pet is left behind. Roger leaves his pet cricket Moe. He leaves a note for Miss Fry saying that Moe likes Miss Fry best. Miss Fry brings the cricket home and makes him her pet.

Ending
Tells how the story ends

Note how the author of this piece:

- Chose the important events from the story. The writer didn't include everything that happened in the story but instead chose the most important parts.

- Used her own words. She did not copy the original story. She also used present tense.

Original: On Parents' Night, the mothers and fathers walked around the classroom with great big smiles on their faces. "Isn't it great," they said, "that Miss Fry loves pets so?"

Summary: On Parents' Night, all the mothers and fathers think it is great that Miss Fry likes pets so much.

110 • Grade 2

Summary • 111

WRITING MODELS AND FORMS

Minilesson 97

Understanding the Summary

Common Core State Standard: W.2.2

Objective: Understand how to use the information presented about the summary.

Guiding Question: How can I use these pages to help me write a good summary?

Teach/Model

Read the definition and bulleted points with children. Add that a summary should not include every detail from the plot, only the most important to understanding the text.

Practice/Apply

Read the model aloud as children read along. Reread the last paragraph. Ask them to describe what happens at the end of the story in their own words.

Minilesson 98

Paraphrasing Text

Common Core State Standard: W.2.2

Objective: Summarize a text in one's own words.

Guiding Question: How do I summarize the details in a text in my own words?

Teach/Model

Explain to children that when they write a summary, they will be describing the most important parts of a text in their own words. Find a brief newspaper article. Paraphrase the first paragraph for children.

Practice/Apply

Read aloud the newspaper article you used in the above activity. Guide children to make suggestions as you summarize the details of the article on the board.

News Story

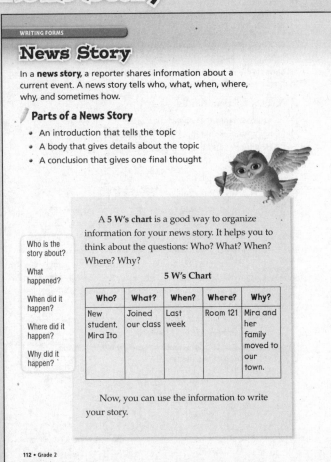

News Story

In a **news story**, a reporter shares information about a current event. A news story tells who, what, when, where, why, and sometimes how.

Parts of a News Story

- An introduction that tells the topic
- A body that gives details about the topic
- A conclusion that gives one final thought

A **5 W's chart** is a good way to organize information for your news story. It helps you to think about the questions: Who? What? When? Where? Why?

Who is the story about?

What happened?

When did it happen?

Where did it happen?

Why did it happen?

5 W's Chart

Who?	What?	When?	Where?	Why?
New student, Mira Ito	Joined our class	Last week	Room 121	Mira and her family moved to our town.

Now, you can use the information to write your story.

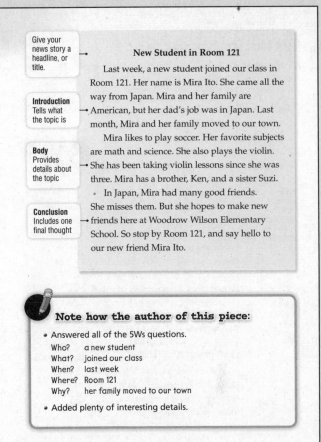

Give your news story a headline, or title.

Introduction
Tells what the topic is

Body
Provides details about the topic

Conclusion
Includes one final thought

New Student in Room 121

Last week, a new student joined our class in Room 121. Her name is Mira Ito. She came all the way from Japan. Mira and her family are American, but her dad's job was in Japan. Last month, Mira and her family moved to our town.

Mira likes to play soccer. Her favorite subjects are math and science. She also plays the violin. She has been taking violin lessons since she was three. Mira has a brother, Ken, and a sister Suzi.

In Japan, Mira had many good friends. She misses them. But she hopes to make new friends here at Woodrow Wilson Elementary School. So stop by Room 121, and say hello to our new friend Mira Ito.

Note how the author of this piece:

- Answered all of the 5Ws questions.
  Who?   a new student
  What?   joined our class
  When?   last week
  Where?   Room 121
  Why?   her family moved to our town
- Added plenty of interesting details.

WRITING MODELS AND FORMS

Minilesson 99

Understanding the News Story

Common Core State Standard: W.2.2

Objective: Understand how to use the information presented about the news story.

Guiding Question: How can I use these pages to help me write a good news story?

Teach/Model

Read the definition and bulleted points with children. Add that the purpose of a news story is to inform the reader. Discuss the 5 W's Chart on p. 112. Explain that the writer used the chart to organize details.

Practice/Apply

Read the model aloud as children read along. Explain to them that the writer added details not found in the chart. Have children identify the added details.

Minilesson 100

Using a 5 W's Chart

Common Core State Standard: W.2.2

Objective: Use a 5 W's chart to write a news story.

Guiding Question: How do I use a 5 W's chart to write a news story?

Teach/Model

With children, review the 5 W's chart on p. 112. Tell them that they can use this chart to gather basic information for their news story.

Practice/Apply

Draw a 5 W's chart on the board. Have children pick a topic for a news story, such as a school event. Write children's suggestions in the chart; then have them use the information in the chart to write full sentences about the news event.

Writing for Science/Writing for Math

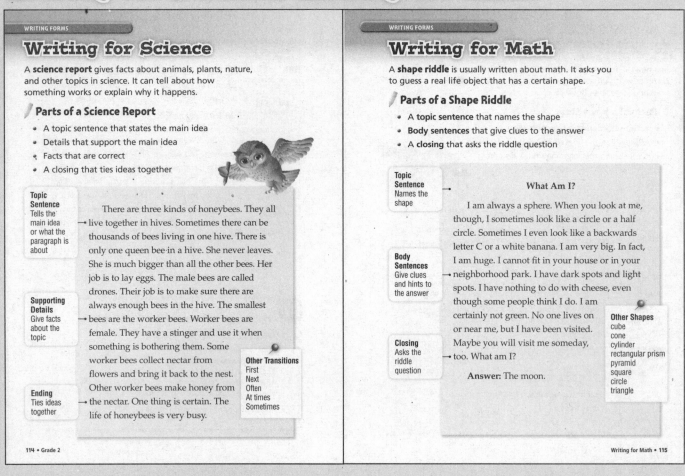

Writing for Science

A **science report** gives facts about animals, plants, nature, and other topics in science. It can tell about how something works or explain why it happens.

Parts of a Science Report

- A topic sentence that states the main idea
- Details that support the main idea
- Facts that are correct
- A closing that ties ideas together

Topic Sentence
Tells the main idea or what the paragraph is about

Supporting Details
Give facts about the topic

Ending
Ties ideas together

There are three kinds of honeybees. They all live together in hives. Sometimes there can be thousands of bees living in one hive. There is only one queen bee in a hive. She never leaves. She is much bigger than all the other bees. Her job is to lay eggs. The male bees are called drones. Their job is to make sure there are always enough bees in the hive. The smallest bees are the worker bees. Worker bees are female. They have a stinger and use it when something is bothering them. Some worker bees collect nectar from flowers and bring it back to the nest. Other worker bees make honey from the nectar. One thing is certain. The life of honeybees is very busy.

Other Transitions
First
Next
Often
At times
Sometimes

Writing for Math

A **shape riddle** is usually written about math. It asks you to guess a real life object that has a certain shape.

Parts of a Shape Riddle

- A topic sentence that names the shape
- Body sentences that give clues to the answer
- A closing that asks the riddle question

Topic Sentence
Names the shape

Body Sentences
Give clues and hints to the answer

Closing
Asks the riddle question

What Am I?

I am always a sphere. When you look at me, though, I sometimes look like a circle or a half circle. Sometimes I even look like a backwards letter C or a white banana. I am very big. In fact, I am huge. I cannot fit in your house or in your neighborhood park. I have dark spots and light spots. I have nothing to do with cheese, even though some people think I do. I am certainly not green. No one lives on or near me, but I have been visited. Maybe you will visit me someday, too. What am I?

Answer: The moon.

Other Shapes
cube
cone
cylinder
rectangular prism
pyramid
square
circle
triangle

WRITING MODELS AND FORMS

Minilesson 101

Understanding Writing for Science

Common Core State Standard: W.2.7

Objective: Understand how to use the information presented about writing for science.

Guiding Question: How can I use these pages to help me write about science?

Teach/Model

Read the definition and bulleted points with children. Explain that science writing is based on facts.

Practice/Apply

Read the model aloud as children read along. Ask children to identify the main idea of the paragraph. Have them discuss other possible science topics for writing.

Minilesson 102

Understanding Writing for Math

Common Core State Standard: W.2.2

Objective: Understand how to use the information presented about writing for math.

Guiding Question: How can I use these pages to help me write about math?

Teach/Model

Read the definition and bulleted points with children. Add that readers should be able to solve the riddle using what they already know as well as the information in the paragraph.

Practice/Apply

Read the model with children. Ask children for an example of another clue that could be included in the shape riddle.

Paragraph That Explains/Recipe

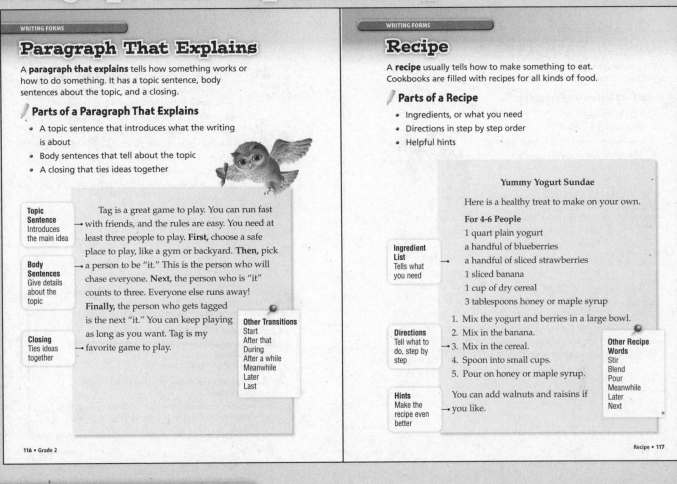

Paragraph That Explains

A **paragraph that explains** tells how something works or how to do something. It has a topic sentence, body sentences about the topic, and a closing.

Parts of a Paragraph That Explains

- A topic sentence that introduces what the writing is about
- Body sentences that tell about the topic
- A closing that ties ideas together

Topic Sentence
Introduces the main idea

Body Sentences
Give details about the topic

Closing
Ties ideas together

Tag is a great game to play. You can run fast with friends, and the rules are easy. You need at least three people to play. **First,** choose a safe place to play, like a gym or backyard. **Then,** pick a person to be "it." This is the person who will chase everyone. **Next,** the person who is "it" counts to three. Everyone else runs away! **Finally,** the person who gets tagged is the next "it." You can keep playing as long as you want. Tag is my favorite game to play.

Other Transitions
Start
After that
During
After a while
Meanwhile
Later
Last

116 • Grade 2

Recipe

A **recipe** usually tells how to make something to eat. Cookbooks are filled with recipes for all kinds of food.

Parts of a Recipe

- Ingredients, or what you need
- Directions in step by step order
- Helpful hints

Yummy Yogurt Sundae

Here is a healthy treat to make on your own.

For 4-6 People
1 quart plain yogurt
a handful of blueberries
a handful of sliced strawberries
1 sliced banana
1 cup of dry cereal
3 tablespoons honey or maple syrup

1. Mix the yogurt and berries in a large bowl.
2. Mix in the banana.
3. Mix in the cereal.
4. Spoon into small cups.
5. Pour on honey or maple syrup.

You can add walnuts and raisins if you like.

Ingredient List
Tells what you need

Directions
Tell what to do, step by step

Hints
Make the recipe even better

Other Recipe Words
Stir
Blend
Pour
Meanwhile
Later
Next

Recipe • 117

WRITING MODELS AND FORMS

Minilesson 103

Understanding the Paragraph That Explains

Common Core State Standard: W.2.2

Objective: Understand how to use the information presented about a paragraph that explains.

Guiding Question: How can I use these pages to help me write a paragraph that explains?

Teach/Model

Read the definition and bulleted points with children. Mention that paragraphs that explain give the readers facts about how something works or how to do something.

Practice/Apply

Read the model with children. Have them identify the topic that the writer wants the reader to learn.

Minilesson 104

Writing a Recipe

Common Core State Standard: W.2.5

Objective: Write a recipe.
Guiding Question: How do I write a recipe?

Teach/Model

Review the model on p. 117. Work with children to brainstorm ideas for another snack they could write a recipe for.

Practice/Apply

Select one of the recipe ideas from the brainstorming session. With children, come up with a list of ingredients. Have them make suggestions as you write the numbered steps on the board. Ask children to come up with helpful hints on their own and share their work with the class.

Writing for Common Core • 95

How-to Paragraph

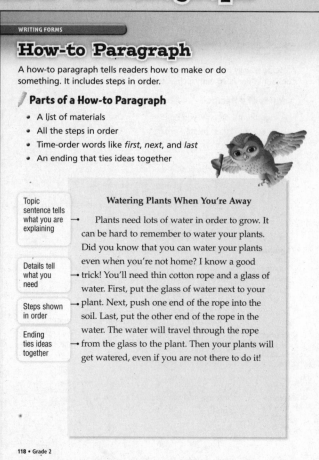

How-to Paragraph

A how-to paragraph tells readers how to make or do something. It includes steps in order.

Parts of a How-to Paragraph

- A list of materials
- All the steps in order
- Time-order words like *first*, *next*, and *last*
- An ending that ties ideas together

Watering Plants When You're Away

Topic sentence tells what you are explaining →

Plants need lots of water in order to grow. It can be hard to remember to water your plants. Did you know that you can water your plants even when you're not home? I know a good

Details tell what you need →

trick! You'll need thin cotton rope and a glass of water. First, put the glass of water next to your

Steps shown in order →

plant. Next, push one end of the rope into the soil. Last, put the other end of the rope in the

Ending ties ideas together →

water. The water will travel through the rope from the glass to the plant. Then your plants will get watered, even if you are not there to do it!

How to Fly a Kite

Topic sentence tells what the paragraph will be about →

I love to fly kites. You can try it, too. You will need a kite, some string, and a windy day. Find a good place with lots of space for running, too. First, stand so the wind is blowing on your back. Then, hold up your kite. When the wind blows,

Steps shown in order →

toss the kite in the air. Next, run and let out some string. Let out more string if the kite goes up. Now you're flying a kite! If the kite crashes,

Closing sentence wraps up the paragraph →

that's okay. Start over and try again. Flying a kite can be really fun!

Note how the author of this piece:

- Explains what the paragraph will be about.
  Did you know that you can water your plants even when you're not home?
  I love to fly kites. You can try it, too.
- Used time-order words like first, next, and then to connect the steps.
  First, stand so the wind is blowing on your back. Then, hold up the kite. Next, run and let out some string.

WRITING MODELS AND FORMS

Minilesson 105

Understanding the How-to Paragraph

Common Core State Standard: W.2.2

Objective: Understand how to use the information presented about a how-to paragraph.

Guiding Question: How can I use these pages to help me write a how-to paragraph?

Teach/Model

Read the definition and bulleted points with children. Tell them that it is important that the steps in a how-to paragraph are presented in a clear, logical order.

Practice/Apply

Read the model on p. 118 aloud as children read along. Have them guide you to rewrite the information in the paragraph as numbered steps on the board.

Minilesson 106

Using Time-Order Words in a How-to Paragraph

Common Core State Standard: W.2.2

Objective: Use time-order words in a how-to paragraph.

Guiding Question: How do I write a how-to paragraph using time-order words?

Teach/Model

Review the model on p. 119. Explain to children that the writer is able to indicate the order of the steps by using time-order words.

Practice/Apply

Have children identify the time-order words used in both models; write these on the board. Have children suggest synonyms for the listed time-order words.

Directions

Directions

Directions tell step-by-step how to do something or get somewhere. Directions use time-order words to help tell what to do. You can use a map to show how to get from one place to another.

Parts of Directions

- A topic sentence about the main idea
- A body with sentences that tell directions in order, step-by-step
- A closing sentence that connects with the main idea

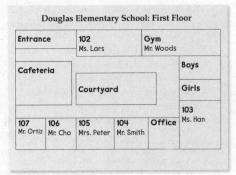

Douglas Elementary School: First Floor

Entrance	102 Ms. Lars	Gym Mr. Woods	
Cafeteria			Boys
	Courtyard		Girls
			103 Ms. Han
107 Mr. Ortiz	106 Mr. Cho	105 Mrs. Peter	104 Mr. Smith	Office

Topic Sentence
Introduces the subject: going to the gym

Body
Tells step-by-step directions in order

Closing Sentence
Connects with the main idea

How to Get to the Gym

→ It is easy to get from Mrs. Peter's room to the gym. First, you start in Mrs. Peter's room. Next, you go out the door into the hallway. Then you turn right. Keep walking until you come to the → office. Then, turn left. Now, walk down the hallway. Pass the courtyard. At the end of the hall, you will see a door. Open the door. → Now, you are in the gym!

Note how the author of this piece:

- Put a title on the directions to make sure readers know what the paragraph is for.
  How to Get to the Gym
- Used time-order words like first, next, and then to connect the steps.
  First, you start in Mrs. Peter's room.
  Next, you go out the door into the hallway.
  Then you turn right.

WRITING MODELS AND FORMS

Minilesson 107

Understanding Directions

Common Core State Standard: W.2.2

Objective: Understand how to use the information presented about directions.

Guiding Question: How can I use these pages to help me write directions?

Teach/Model

Read the definition and bulleted points with children. Tell children that directions can sometimes include a graphic, such as a map, to illustrate steps in the directions.

Practice/Apply

Read the model aloud. Have children trace the directions on the map with a pencil or their fingers. Discuss how the map helps make the directions clear.

Minilesson 108

Writing Directions

Common Core State Standard: W.2.2

Objective: Write a paragraph that includes directions.

Guiding Question: How do I write a paragraph that includes directions?

Teach/Model

Go over the model on p. 121. Point out to children how the writer uses transitions to make the directions easy to follow. Discuss how children might write directions from your classroom to another place in the school.

Practice/Apply

With children, write a paragraph giving directions from your classroom to the location you chose. If possible, sketch a map on the board.

Paragraph That Compares/Paragraph That Contrasts

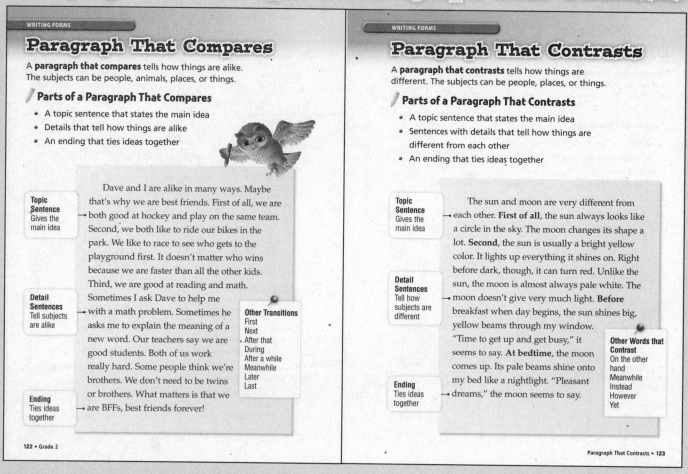

WRITING FORMS

Paragraph That Compares

A **paragraph that compares** tells how things are alike. The subjects can be people, animals, places, or things.

Parts of a Paragraph That Compares

- A topic sentence that states the main idea
- Details that tell how things are alike
- An ending that ties ideas together

Topic Sentence Gives the main idea

Dave and I are alike in many ways. Maybe that's why we are best friends. First of all, we are both good at hockey and play on the same team. Second, we both like to ride our bikes in the park. We like to race to see who gets to the playground first. It doesn't matter who wins because we are faster than all the other kids. Third, we are good at reading and math.

Detail Sentences Tell subjects are alike

Sometimes I ask Dave to help me with a math problem. Sometimes he asks me to explain the meaning of a new word. Our teachers say we are good students. Both of us work really hard. Some people think we're brothers. We don't need to be twins or brothers. What matters is that we

Ending Ties ideas together

are BFFs, best friends forever!

Other Transitions
First
Next
After that
During
After a while
Meanwhile
Later
Last

122 • Grade 2

WRITING FORMS

Paragraph That Contrasts

A **paragraph that contrasts** tells how things are different. The subjects can be people, places, or things.

Parts of a Paragraph That Contrasts

- A topic sentence that states the main idea
- Sentences with details that tell how things are different from each other
- An ending that ties ideas together

Topic Sentence Gives the main idea

The sun and moon are very different from each other. **First of all**, the sun always looks like a circle in the sky. The moon changes its shape a lot. **Second**, the sun is usually a bright yellow color. It lights up everything it shines on. Right before dark, though, it can turn red. Unlike the sun, the moon is almost always pale white. The

Detail Sentences Tell how subjects are different

moon doesn't give very much light. **Before** breakfast when day begins, the sun shines big, yellow beams through my window. "Time to get up and get busy," it seems to say. **At bedtime**, the moon comes up. Its pale beams shine onto

Ending Ties ideas together

my bed like a nightlight. "Pleasant dreams," the moon seems to say.

Other Words that Contrast
On the other hand
Meanwhile
Instead
However
Yet

Paragraph That Contrasts • 123

WRITING MODELS AND FORMS

Minilesson 109

Understanding the Paragraph That Compares

Common Core State Standard: W.2.2

Objective: Understand how to use the information presented about a paragraph that compares.

Guiding Question: How can I use these pages to help me write a paragraph that compares?

Teach/Model

Read the definition and bulleted points with children. Tell them that usually, two things can be compared even if they seem very different.

Practice/Apply

Read the model aloud with children. Have them identify the ways that the writer says that he and Dave are alike.

Minilesson 110

Understanding the Paragraph That Contrasts

Common Core State Standard: W.2.2

Objective: Understand how to use the information presented about a paragraph that contrasts.

Guiding Question: How can I use these pages to help me write a paragraph that contrasts?

Teach/Model

Read the definition and bulleted points with children. Tell them that contrasts are differences. Give examples of sentences containing contrasts.

Practice/Apply

Read the model on p. 123. Go over the box with contrast words. Have children come up with other words that can be used to show contrast.

Research Report

WRITING FORMS

Research Report

A **research report** uses your own words to give information about a topic.

Parts of a Research Report

- An introduction that tells the main idea—what the report is about
- A body with facts and details about the main idea
- A graph, diagram, or chart, if needed
- A conclusion that sums up the report

Introduction
Tells the main idea—what the report is about

Details tell what the Big Dipper looks like.

Body
Tells facts and details about the main idea

The Big Dipper

Look up at the stars. See if you can find the Big Dipper. It looks like a big soup ladle made out of stars.

Constellations are groups of stars that look like pictures in the sky. The Big Dipper looks like the ladle you use to lift soup out of a pot. It is part of a constellation called Ursa Major.

There are seven stars in the Big Dipper, and each star has a name. The names are Alkaid, Mizar, Alioth, Megrez, Phecda, Merak, and Dubhe.

The Big Dipper is a helpful group of stars. For example, it can help you find the North Star. The stars on the end of the Big Dipper's bowl

Examples help make a report more interesting.

Conclusion Sums up the main idea

point to the North Star. The North Star shows which direction is north. The Big Dipper is also helpful for finding another picture in the sky. First, use the Big Dipper to find the North Star. Then look to the left of the North Star. You will see the Little Dipper. The end of its handle is the North Star.

Some other names for the Big Dipper are the Big Bear, the Saucepan, and the Plough. Many years ago, some called it The Drinking Gourd.

The Big Dipper is a very interesting group of stars. It is one of many pictures in the night sky.

Note how the author of this piece:

- Used words to describe the Big Dipper.
  The Big Dipper looks like the ladle that you use to lift soup out of a pot.
- Could have used a diagram. Instead of just describing the Big Dipper, the author might have included a photo or drawing of it. That would help the reader see what the author is describing.

124 • Grade 2

Research Report • 125

WRITING MODELS AND FORMS

Minilesson 111

Introducing a Research Report

Common Core State Standard: W.2.2

Objective: Understand how to write a research report.
Guiding Question: How do I write a research report?

Teach/Model

With children, read pp. 124–125. Tell children that a research report uses details, pictures, examples, and clear organization to explain a topic to the reader.

Practice/Apply

Discuss the student model. Ask children to point out facts and examples included in the report. Have them suggest ideas for diagrams that the author could have included.

Minilesson 112

Understanding Details in a Research Report

Common Core State Standard: W.2.2

Objective: Understand how details contribute to a research report.
Guiding Question: How do details support my research report?

Teach/Model

Review pp. 124–125. Explain to children that a research report must use details and examples to support the main idea.

Practice/Apply

Have children point out the main idea in each paragraph, such as what the Big Dipper looks like or why the Big Dipper is helpful. Then ask them to discuss the details in each paragraph that explain and support the main idea.

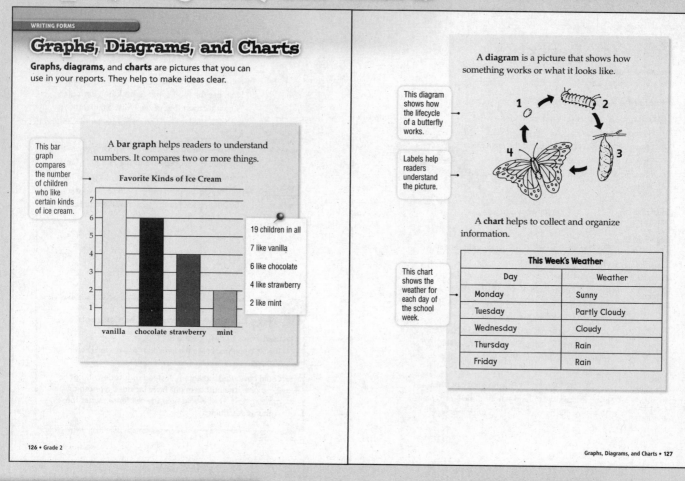

Graphs, Diagrams, and Charts

Graphs, diagrams, and **charts** are pictures that you can use in your reports. They help to make ideas clear.

This bar graph compares the number of children who like certain kinds of ice cream.

A **bar graph** helps readers to understand numbers. It compares two or more things.

Favorite Kinds of Ice Cream

19 children in all

7 like vanilla

6 like chocolate

4 like strawberry

2 like mint

vanilla   chocolate   strawberry   mint

A **diagram** is a picture that shows how something works or what it looks like.

This diagram shows how the lifecycle of a butterfly works.

Labels help readers understand the picture.

A **chart** helps to collect and organize information.

This chart shows the weather for each day of the school week.

This Week's Weather	
Day	Weather
Monday	Sunny
Tuesday	Partly Cloudy
Wednesday	Cloudy
Thursday	Rain
Friday	Rain

WRITING MODELS AND FORMS

Minilesson 113

Introducing Graphs, Diagrams, and Charts

Common Core State Standard: W.2.2

Objective: Understand how graphs, diagrams, and charts work.

Guiding Question: How do I choose from among graphs, diagrams, and charts?

Teach/Model

Read pp. 126–127. Point out the differences between the examples. Explain that a research topic and the point the writer wants to make will determine which visual to use.

Practice/Apply

Ask children which picture would be best for collecting daily observations of plant growth? Which would be best for showing the parts of a plant?

Minilesson 114

Using Graphs, Diagrams, and Charts in a Report

Common Core State Standard: W.2.2

Objective: Understand how to create and use a graph, diagram, or chart in a research report.

Guiding Question: How do I include a graph, diagram, or chart in my research report?

Teach/Model

Review pp. 126–127. Remind children that charts and diagrams help readers understand information.

Practice/Apply

Ask children what kind of graphic would work on a report about pets. Have them create a graph, diagram, or chart that shows the number or type of pets owned by the children in the class.

Multimedia Report

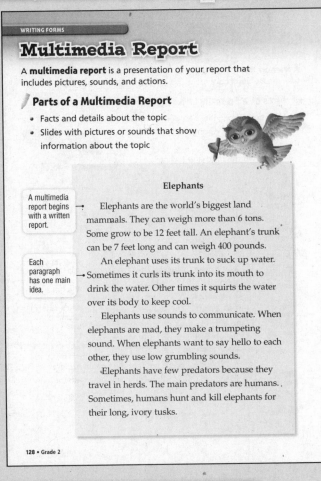

Multimedia Report

A **multimedia report** is a presentation of your report that includes pictures, sounds, and actions.

Parts of a Multimedia Report

- Facts and details about the topic
- Slides with pictures or sounds that show information about the topic

Elephants

A multimedia report begins with a written report.

Each paragraph has one main idea.

Elephants are the world's biggest land mammals. They can weigh more than 6 tons. Some grow to be 12 feet tall. An elephant's trunk can be 7 feet long and can weigh 400 pounds.

An elephant uses its trunk to suck up water. Sometimes it curls its trunk into its mouth to drink the water. Other times it squirts the water over its body to keep cool.

Elephants use sounds to communicate. When elephants are mad, they make a trumpeting sound. When elephants want to say hello to each other, they use low grumbling sounds.

Elephants have few predators because they travel in herds. The main predators are humans. Sometimes, humans hunt and kill elephants for their long, ivory tusks.

128 • Grade 2

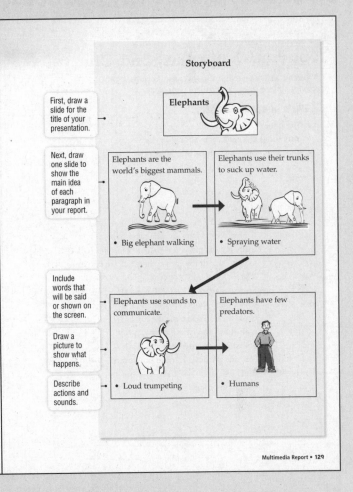

Storyboard

First, draw a slide for the title of your presentation.

Next, draw one slide to show the main idea of each paragraph in your report.

Include words that will be said or shown on the screen.

Draw a picture to show what happens.

Describe actions and sounds.

Elephants

Elephants are the world's biggest mammals.
- Big elephant walking

Elephants use their trunks to suck up water.
- Spraying water

Elephants use sounds to communicate.
- Loud trumpeting

Elephants have few predators.
- Humans

Multimedia Report • 129

Minilesson 115

Introducing the Multimedia Report

Common Core State Standard: W.2.6

Objective: Understand how a multimedia report conveys information.

Guiding Question: How do multimedia reports convey information?

Teach/Model

Read pp. 128–129. Explain that a multimedia report uses more than words—such as pictures and sounds—to tell about something.

Practice/Apply

Ask children to discuss the differences and the connections between the written text and the storyboard. Ask children how the two parts work together to offer information about elephants.

Minilesson 116

Using Media in a Report

Common Core State Standard: W.2.6

Objective: Understand how to use multimedia in a report.

Guiding Question: How do I use images, sound, or movies in a multimedia report?

Teach/Model

Review pp. 128–129. Remind children that a multimedia report uses more than words to provide a full understanding of a topic.

Practice/Apply

Ask children to plan a storyboard about a familiar instrument, such as a piano or guitar. Ask them to include at least three pictures and one other type of media (such as sound or video) to enrich the report.

Journal/Friendly Letter

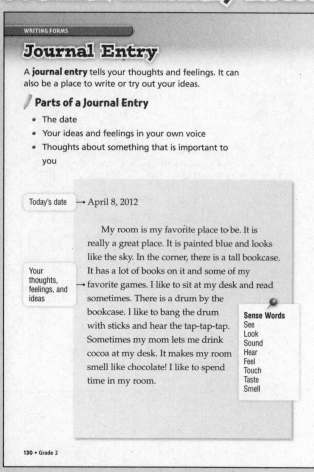

Journal Entry

A **journal entry** tells your thoughts and feelings. It can also be a place to write or try out your ideas.

Parts of a Journal Entry
- The date
- Your ideas and feelings in your own voice
- Thoughts about something that is important to you

Today's date → April 8, 2012

Your thoughts, feelings, and ideas →

My room is my favorite place to be. It is really a great place. It is painted blue and looks like the sky. In the corner, there is a tall bookcase. It has a lot of books on it and some of my favorite games. I like to sit at my desk and read sometimes. There is a drum by the bookcase. I like to bang the drum with sticks and hear the tap-tap-tap. Sometimes my mom lets me drink cocoa at my desk. It makes my room smell like chocolate! I like to spend time in my room.

Sense Words
See
Look
Sound
Hear
Feel
Touch
Taste
Smell

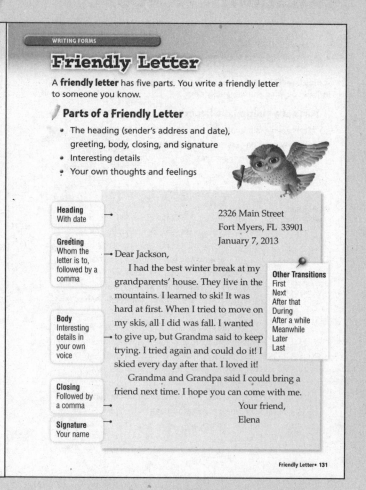

Friendly Letter

A **friendly letter** has five parts. You write a friendly letter to someone you know.

Parts of a Friendly Letter
- The heading (sender's address and date), greeting, body, closing, and signature
- Interesting details
- Your own thoughts and feelings

Heading With date →

2326 Main Street
Fort Myers, FL 33901
January 7, 2013

Greeting Whom the letter is to, followed by a comma →

Dear Jackson,

Body Interesting details in your own voice →

I had the best winter break at my grandparents' house. They live in the mountains. I learned to ski! It was hard at first. When I tried to move on my skis, all I did was fall. I wanted to give up, but Grandma said to keep trying. I tried again and could do it! I skied every day after that. I loved it!

Grandma and Grandpa said I could bring a friend next time. I hope you can come with me.

Other Transitions
First
Next
After that
During
After a while
Meanwhile
Later
Last

Closing Followed by a comma →

Your friend,

Signature Your name →

Elena

WRITING MODELS AND FORMS

Minilesson 117

Introducing the Journal

Common Core State Standard: W.2.2

Objective: Understand how to write journal entries.

Guiding Question: How do I write journal entries?

Teach/Model

Read p. 130. Explain to children that a journal is a way for them to write only for themselves. With a journal, a writer can practice storytelling or express feelings.

Practice/Apply

Ask children to compose a short journal entry. Have them write the date at the top, and ask them to write about writing: what part of the writing process comes easily to them, what challenges them, and what kind of writing entertains them.

Minilesson 118

Introducing the Friendly Letter

Common Core State Standard: W.2.2

Objective: Understand how to write friendly letters.

Guiding Question: How do I write friendly letters?

Teach/Model

Read p. 131. Point out the parts of a friendly letter in the student model. Explain that writing a friendly letter is one way for people to share interesting details about something that happened to them.

Practice/Apply

Ask children to compose a friendly letter to a family member telling about events from a recent school activity. Have them include all the parts of a friendly letter.

Invitation/Envelope

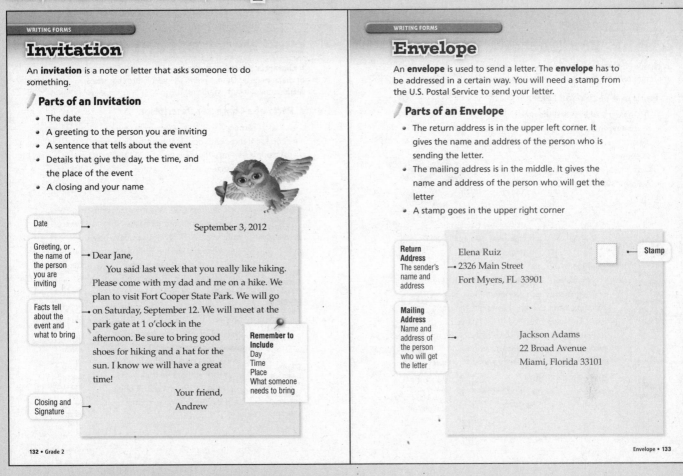

Invitation

WRITING FORMS

An **invitation** is a note or letter that asks someone to do something.

Parts of an Invitation

- The date
- A greeting to the person you are inviting
- A sentence that tells about the event
- Details that give the day, the time, and the place of the event
- A closing and your name

Date

Greeting, or the name of the person you are inviting

Facts tell about the event and what to bring

Closing and Signature

September 3, 2012

Dear Jane,

You said last week that you really like hiking. Please come with my dad and me on a hike. We plan to visit Fort Cooper State Park. We will go on Saturday, September 12. We will meet at the park gate at 1 o'clock in the afternoon. Be sure to bring good shoes for hiking and a hat for the sun. I know we will have a great time!

Your friend,
Andrew

Remember to Include
Day
Time
Place
What someone needs to bring

132 • Grade 2

Envelope

WRITING FORMS

An **envelope** is used to send a letter. The **envelope** has to be addressed in a certain way. You will need a stamp from the U.S. Postal Service to send your letter.

Parts of an Envelope

- The return address is in the upper left corner. It gives the name and address of the person who is sending the letter.
- The mailing address is in the middle. It gives the name and address of the person who will get the letter
- A stamp goes in the upper right corner

Return Address
The sender's name and address

Mailing Address
Name and address of the person who will get the letter

Elena Ruiz
2326 Main Street
Fort Myers, FL 33901

Stamp

Jackson Adams
22 Broad Avenue
Miami, Florida 33101

Envelope • 133

WRITING MODELS AND FORMS

Minilesson 119

Introducing the Invitation

Common Core State Standard: W.2.2

Objective: Understand how to write invitations.
Guiding Question: How do I write an invitation?

Teach/Model

Read p. 132. Explain to children that an invitation asks someone to join you in a fun activity or event. Point out that the language in an invitation usually shows enthusiasm, making the reader want to attend the event.

Practice/Apply

Ask children to write an invitation that invites friends to their fantasy birthday party. Have them include all the parts of an invitation while keeping the language vivid.

Minilesson 120

Introducing the Envelope

Common Core State Standard: W.2.2

Objective: Understand how to address an envelope.
Guiding Question: How do I address an envelope?

Teach/Model

Read p. 133. Point out that the remaining space on the front of an envelope should stay empty of words so that the envelope can be easily read and sorted in the mail.

Practice/Apply

Ask children to address an envelope using all of the parts identified on p. 133. Ask them to discuss what kind of correspondence they might put inside such an envelope—for example, a friendly letter or an invitation.

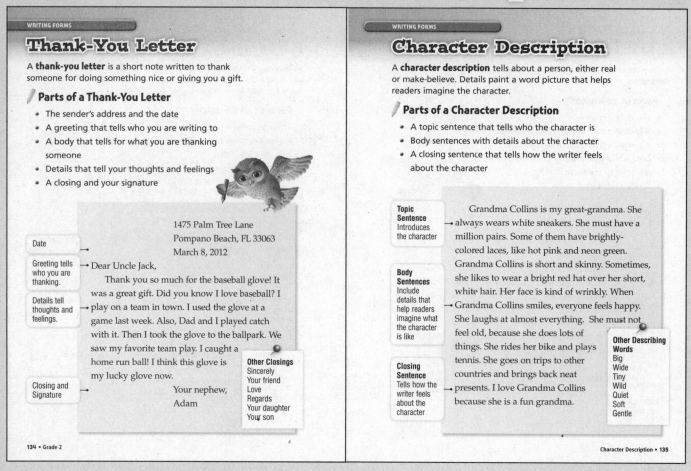

Thank-You Letter/Character Description

Minilesson 121

Introducing the Thank-You Letter

Common Core State Standard: W.2.2

Objective: Understand how to write thank-you letters.

Guiding Question: How do I write a thank-you letter?

Teach/Model

Read p. 134. Point out the parts of a thank-you letter in the student model. Explain to children that the closing they use should match the kind of relationship the writer shares with the recipient of the letter and the kind gesture the recipient made.

Practice/Apply

Ask children to write a thank-you letter to someone who recently did something nice for them or for someone they know. Have children include all parts of a thank-you letter, including an appropriate closing.

Minilesson 122

Introducing the Character Description

Common Core State Standard: W.2.2

Objective: Understand how to write a character description.

Guiding Question: How do I write a character description?

Teach/Model

Read p. 135. Explain to children that a character description usually includes details that make the character unique. Writers often include their feelings when writing about a character or person they know.

Practice/Apply

Ask children to write a brief description about a character from a story they recently read. Encourage children to include descriptive words like the ones on p. 135 to make their work and the character vivid.

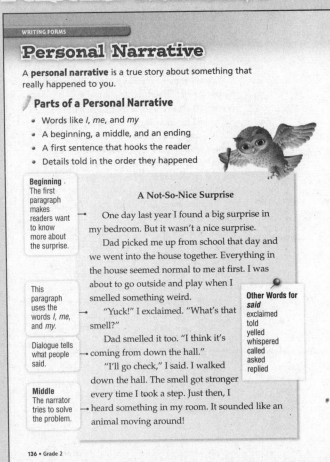

Personal Narrative

Personal Narrative

A **personal narrative** is a true story about something that really happened to you.

Parts of a Personal Narrative

- Words like *I*, *me*, and *my*
- A beginning, a middle, and an ending
- A first sentence that hooks the reader
- Details told in the order they happened

Beginning
The first paragraph makes readers want to know more about the surprise.

This paragraph uses the words *I*, *me*, and *my*.

Dialogue tells what people said.

Middle
The narrator tries to solve the problem.

A Not-So-Nice Surprise

One day last year I found a big surprise in my bedroom. But it wasn't a nice surprise.

Dad picked me up from school that day and we went into the house together. Everything in the house seemed normal to me at first. I was about to go outside and play when I smelled something weird.

"Yuck!" I exclaimed. "What's that smell?"

Dad smelled it too. "I think it's coming from down the hall."

"I'll go check," I said. I walked down the hall. The smell got stronger every time I took a step. Just then, I heard something in my room. It sounded like an animal moving around!

Other Words for *said*
exclaimed
told
yelled
whispered
called
asked
replied

These paragraphs tell details in time order.

This paragraph makes the reader even more curious. What could the animal be?

I looked in. I saw a black cat with a white stripe sitting on the floor. There was just one problem. We didn't have a cat!

Then the animal looked at me and I saw what it was. It wasn't a cat. It was a skunk!

Dad called a man named Mr. Todd who had a special skunk trap. He trapped the skunk and let it go in the woods. He said I was smart not to try to catch the skunk myself.

Ending
The final paragraphs show how the family solved the problem.

We left the window of my bedroom open for two days. We also washed my sheets and blankets—twice! For a while I slept in my sleeping bag on the living room floor. That was cool! But finally the smell was gone! We were glad.

Note how the author of this piece:

- Used details to build suspense.
  Just then, I heard something in my room. It sounded like an animal moving around!
- Gave information about when the event took place.
  One day last year I found a big surprise in my bedroom.

Minilesson 123

Introducing the Personal Narrative

Common Core State Standard: W.2.3

Objective: Understand how to write a personal narrative.

Guiding Question: How do I write a personal narrative?

Teach/Model

Read pp. 136–137. Explain that a personal narrative doesn't simply describe something true about the writer but tells a story with a beginning, middle, and end. Point out that a personal narrative may include people other than the writer.

Practice/Apply

Have children identify the beginning, middle, and end of the narrative. Ask them to name the characters and discuss why they are important to the narrative.

Minilesson 124

Using Dialogue in a Personal Narrative

Common Core State Standard: W.2.3

Objective: Use dialogue in a personal narrative.

Guiding Question: How do I write dialogue?

Teach/Model

Review pp. 136–137. Explain to children that a personal narrative usually includes dialogue between the people involved in the narrative's events. Show children the *Other Words for said* box and discuss the differences among those words.

Practice/Apply

Guide children to write dialogue for a true event that the class has experienced, such as a field trip. Encourage them to use words in the *Other Words for said* box.

Writing for Common Core • **105**

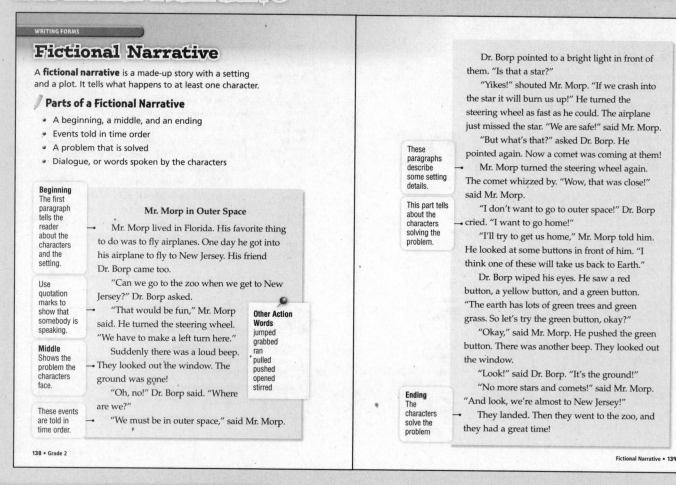

Fictional Narrative

WRITING FORMS

Fictional Narrative

A **fictional narrative** is a made-up story with a setting and a plot. It tells what happens to at least one character.

Parts of a Fictional Narrative

- A beginning, a middle, and an ending
- Events told in time order
- A problem that is solved
- Dialogue, or words spoken by the characters

Beginning
The first paragraph tells the reader about the characters and the setting.

Use quotation marks to show that somebody is speaking.

Middle
Shows the problem the characters face.

These events are told in time order.

Mr. Morp in Outer Space

Mr. Morp lived in Florida. His favorite thing to do was to fly airplanes. One day he got into his airplane to fly to New Jersey. His friend Dr. Borp came too.

"Can we go to the zoo when we get to New Jersey?" Dr. Borp asked.

"That would be fun," Mr. Morp said. He turned the steering wheel. "We have to make a left turn here."

Suddenly there was a loud beep. They looked out the window. The ground was gone!

"Oh, no!" Dr. Borp said. "Where are we?"

"We must be in outer space," said Mr. Morp.

Other Action Words
jumped
grabbed
ran
pulled
pushed
opened
stirred

These paragraphs describe some setting details.

This part tells about the characters solving the problem.

Dr. Borp pointed to a bright light in front of them. "Is that a star?"

"Yikes!" shouted Mr. Morp. "If we crash into the star it will burn us up!" He turned the steering wheel as fast as he could. The airplane just missed the star. "We are safe!" said Mr. Morp.

"But what's that?" asked Dr. Borp. He pointed again. Now a comet was coming at them!

Mr. Morp turned the steering wheel again. The comet whizzed by. "Wow, that was close!" said Mr. Morp.

"I don't want to go to outer space!" Dr. Borp cried. "I want to go home!"

"I'll try to get us home," Mr. Morp told him. He looked at some buttons in front of him. "I think one of these will take us back to Earth."

Dr. Borp wiped his eyes. He saw a red button, a yellow button, and a green button. "The earth has lots of green trees and green grass. So let's try the green button, okay?"

"Okay," said Mr. Morp. He pushed the green button. There was another beep. They looked out the window.

"Look!" said Dr. Borp. "It's the ground!"

"No more stars and comets!" said Mr. Morp. "And look, we're almost to New Jersey!"

They landed. Then they went to the zoo, and they had a great time!

Ending
The characters solve the problem

138 • Grade 2

Fictional Narrative • 139

WRITING MODELS AND FORMS

Minilesson 125

Introducing the Fictional Narrative

Common Core State Standard: W.2.3

Objective: Understand how to plan a fictional narrative.

Guiding Question: How do I plan a fictional narrative?

Teach/Model

Read pp. 138–139. Explain that the plot in a fictional narrative is a made-up series of events. The story happens in a specific setting, or time and place, and the characters have a problem to solve.

Practice/Apply

Ask children to create a setting for a fictional narrative, as well as characters with a problem to solve. For example, *a school; two friends try out for the same part in the class play.* Have them brainstorm and list their ideas on paper.

Minilesson 126

Using Dialogue in a Fictional Narrative

Common Core State Standard: W.2.3

Objective: Understand how to write dialogue in a fictional narrative.

Guiding Question: How do I write dialogue in a fictional narrative?

Teach/Model

Review the model. Explain to children that dialogue makes the action in a fictional narrative seem more real. Point out the dialogue punctuation.

Practice/Apply

Ask children to write dialogue for the characters they created in Minilesson 125. Remind them that dialogue should sound like the way people actually talk. Check that they use quotation marks and commas correctly.

Fairy Tale

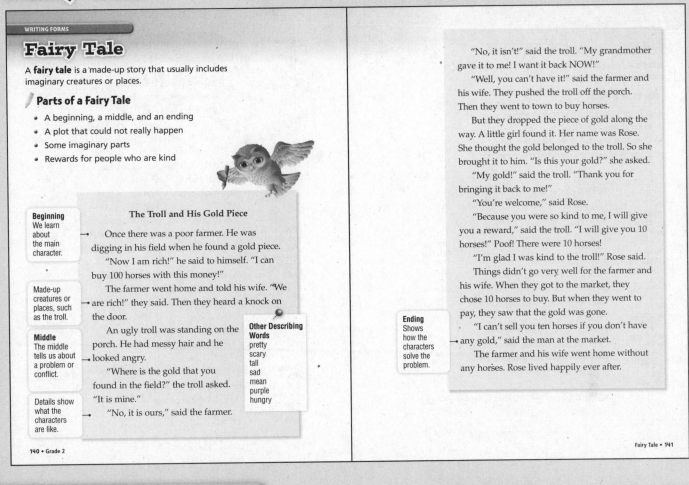

Fairy Tale

A **fairy tale** is a made-up story that usually includes imaginary creatures or places.

Parts of a Fairy Tale

- A beginning, a middle, and an ending
- A plot that could not really happen
- Some imaginary parts
- Rewards for people who are kind

Beginning
We learn about the main character.

Made-up creatures or places, such as the troll.

Middle
The middle tells us about a problem or conflict.

Details show what the characters are like.

The Troll and His Gold Piece

Once there was a poor farmer. He was digging in his field when he found a gold piece.

"Now I am rich!" he said to himself. "I can buy 100 horses with this money!"

The farmer went home and told his wife. "We are rich!" they said. Then they heard a knock on the door.

An ugly troll was standing on the porch. He had messy hair and he looked angry.

"Where is the gold that you found in the field?" the troll asked. "It is mine."

"No, it is ours," said the farmer.

Other Describing Words
pretty
scary
tall
sad
mean
purple
hungry

"No, it isn't!" said the troll. "My grandmother gave it to me! I want it back NOW!"

"Well, you can't have it!" said the farmer and his wife. They pushed the troll off the porch. Then they went to town to buy horses.

But they dropped the piece of gold along the way. A little girl found it. Her name was Rose. She thought the gold belonged to the troll. So she brought it to him. "Is this your gold?" she asked.

"My gold!" said the troll. "Thank you for bringing it back to me!"

"You're welcome," said Rose.

"Because you were so kind to me, I will give you a reward," said the troll. "I will give you 10 horses!" Poof! There were 10 horses!

"I'm glad I was kind to the troll!" Rose said.

Things didn't go very well for the farmer and his wife. When they got to the market, they chose 10 horses to buy. But when they went to pay, they saw that the gold was gone.

"I can't sell you ten horses if you don't have any gold," said the man at the market.

The farmer and his wife went home without any horses. Rose lived happily ever after.

Ending
Shows how the characters solve the problem.

140 • Grade 2

Fairy Tale • 141

WRITING MODELS AND FORMS

Minilesson 127

Introducing the Fairy Tale

Common Core State Standard: W.2.3

Objective: Understand how to plan a fairy tale.

Guiding Question: How do I plan a fairy tale?

Teach/Model

Read pp. 140–141. Point out to children that the plot has a beginning, middle, and end. In fairy tales, there are often magical creatures or unusual events. Ask children to name some other fairy tales they know.

Practice/Apply

Ask children to plan the plot of a fairy tale. Have them invent a magical creature whose powers are used to alter the plot.

Minilesson 128

Using Details in a Fairy Tale

Common Core State Standard: W.2.3

Objective: Understand how to use details in a fairy tale.

Guiding Question: How do I use details to create a vivid fairy tale?

Teach/Model

Review pp. 140–141. Point out to children the vivid word choices in the student model, such as *poor, ugly,* and *messy.* Explain that details such as these make a fairy tale exciting and interesting.

Practice/Apply

Ask children to use their planned plot from Minilesson 127 to write a brief fairy tale. Have them include descriptive words, such as those in the *Other Describing Words* box.

Play

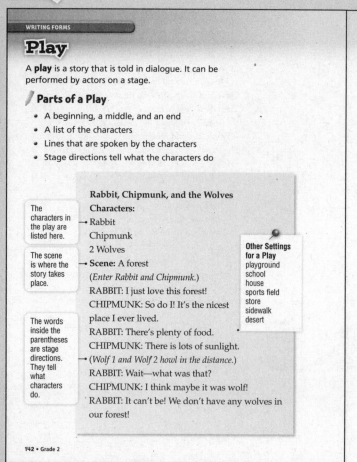

Play

A **play** is a story that is told in dialogue. It can be performed by actors on a stage.

Parts of a Play

- A beginning, a middle, and an end
- A list of the characters
- Lines that are spoken by the characters
- Stage directions tell what the characters do

The characters in the play are listed here.

The scene is where the story takes place.

The words inside the parentheses are stage directions. They tell what characters do.

Rabbit, Chipmunk, and the Wolves

Characters:
Rabbit
Chipmunk
2 Wolves
Scene: A forest
(*Enter Rabbit and Chipmunk.*)
RABBIT: I just love this forest!
CHIPMUNK: So do I! It's the nicest place I ever lived.
RABBIT: There's plenty of food.
CHIPMUNK: There is lots of sunlight.
(*Wolf 1 and Wolf 2 howl in the distance.*)
RABBIT: Wait—what was that?
CHIPMUNK: I think maybe it was wolf!
RABBIT: It can't be! We don't have any wolves in our forest!

Other Settings for a Play
playground
school
house
sports field
store
sidewalk
desert

142 • Grade 2

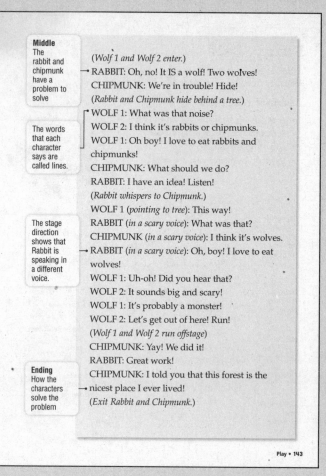

Middle
The rabbit and chipmunk have a problem to solve

The words that each character says are called lines.

The stage direction shows that Rabbit is speaking in a different voice.

Ending
How the characters solve the problem

(*Wolf 1 and Wolf 2 enter.*)
RABBIT: Oh, no! It IS a wolf! Two wolves!
CHIPMUNK: We're in trouble! Hide!
(*Rabbit and Chipmunk hide behind a tree.*)
WOLF 1: What was that noise?
WOLF 2: I think it's rabbits or chipmunks.
WOLF 1: Oh boy! I love to eat rabbits and chipmunks!
CHIPMUNK: What should we do?
RABBIT: I have an idea! Listen!
(*Rabbit whispers to Chipmunk.*)
WOLF 1 (*pointing to tree*): This way!
RABBIT (*in a scary voice*): What was that?
CHIPMUNK (*in a scary voice*): I think it's wolves.
RABBIT (*in a scary voice*): Oh, boy! I love to eat wolves!
WOLF 1: Uh-oh! Did you hear that?
WOLF 2: It sounds big and scary!
WOLF 1: It's probably a monster!
WOLF 2: Let's get out of here! Run!
(*Wolf 1 and Wolf 2 run offstage*)
CHIPMUNK: Yay! We did it!
RABBIT: Great work!
CHIPMUNK: I told you that this forest is the nicest place I ever lived!
(*Exit Rabbit and Chipmunk.*)

Play • 143

WRITING MODELS AND FORMS

Minilesson 129

Introducing the Play

Common Core State Standard: W.2.3

Objective: Understand how to write a play.

Guiding Question: How do I write a play?

Teach/Model

Together, read pp. 142–143. Explain to children that, in a play, information that the audience needs to know comes primarily through the characters. They say and do the things that move the plot forward.

Practice/Apply

Have children discuss how different characters affect the plot. Ask them how the play would change if, for example, the rabbit were not in the play. Discuss how the play would be different without the wolves.

Minilesson 130

Using Stage Directions in a Play

Common Core State Standard: W.2.3

Objective: Understand how to use stage directions in a play.

Guiding Question: How do I use stage directions to add clarity to a play?

Teach/Model

Point out to children the stage direction on p. 143 that reads "(*Rabbit and Chipmunk hide behind a tree.*)" Explain to children that stage directions tell actors what to do and allow readers to envision what is happening on stage.

Practice/Apply

Ask children to discuss the stage directions throughout the play. Ask them to explain how each stage direction adds clarity to the play.

Poems

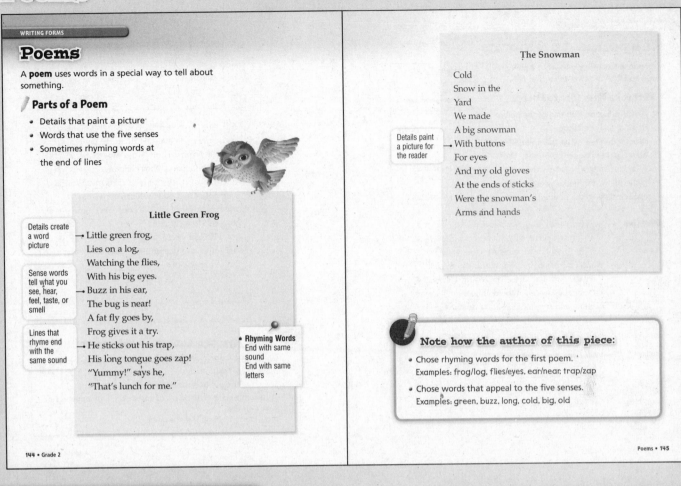

Poems

A **poem** uses words in a special way to tell about something.

Parts of a Poem

- Details that paint a picture
- Words that use the five senses
- Sometimes rhyming words at the end of lines

Details create a word picture →

Sense words tell what you see, hear, feel, taste, or smell →

Lines that rhyme end with the same sound →

Little Green Frog

Little green frog,
Lies on a log,
Watching the flies,
With his big eyes.
Buzz in his ear,
The bug is near!
A fat fly goes by,
Frog gives it a try.
He sticks out his trap,
His long tongue goes zap!
"Yummy!" says he,
"That's lunch for me."

- **Rhyming Words**
  End with same sound
  End with same letters

144 • Grade 2

The Snowman

Cold
Snow in the
Yard
We made
A big snowman
→ With buttons
For eyes
And my old gloves
At the ends of sticks
Were the snowman's
Arms and hands

Details paint a picture for the reader →

Note how the author of this piece:

- Chose rhyming words for the first poem.
  Examples: frog/log, flies/eyes, ear/near, trap/zap
- Chose words that appeal to the five senses.
  Examples: green, buzz, long, cold, big, old

Poems • 145

WRITING MODELS AND FORMS

Minilesson 131

Introducing Poems

Common Core State Standard: W.2.3

Objective: Understand how poems convey ideas.

Guiding Question: How do poems convey ideas to readers?

Teach/Model

Read pp. 144–145. Explain to children that though poems use relatively few words, they contain vivid details. Poets use sense words to help readers imagine events or characters in their poems.

Practice/Apply

Have children discuss the poems on pp. 144–145. Ask them to draw a picture that includes all of the details in one of the poems. Ask children to discuss the number of details they found in the few words used by each poet.

Minilesson 132

Using Rhyme in Poems

Common Core State Standard: W.2.3

Objective: Understand how to use rhyme in a poem.

Guiding Question: How do I use rhyme to make my poem interesting?

Teach/Model

Point out to children the rhyming words in the poem on p. 144. Read the *Rhyming Words* box beside the student model. Tell children that rhyming lines can occur in patterns, like in the rhyming pairs in this poem.

Practice/Apply

Ask children to create a list of rhyming pairs like the ones in *Little Green Frog.* Have them choose words that relate to one topic. Then, challenge children to write a brief poem using those rhyming words.

Response to Poetry

WRITING FORMS

Response to Poetry

A **response to poetry** tells what a poem is about and how it makes the writer feel.

Parts of a Response to Poetry

- An introduction that names the poem, its kind, and the author
- A body that tells what the poem is about and the writer's thoughts
- A conclusion that tells how the poem made the writer feel or why the writer liked or disliked the poem

Autumn Fires

In the other gardens
And all up the vale,
From the autumn bonfires
See the smoke trail!

Pleasant summer over
And all the summer flowers,
The red fire blazes,
The grey smoke towers.

Sing a song of seasons!
Something bright in all!
Flowers in the summer,
Fires in the fall!

—*Robert Louis Stevenson*

Introduction
Names the poem and its author

Body
Tells what the poem is about and includes the writer's thoughts about the poem

Ending
Tells how the poem made the writer feel

I read a rhyming poem called "Autumn Fires." It was written by Robert Louis Stevenson.

"Autumn Fires" paints a picture with words. It is about bonfires burning in the fall. I like the part that says, "The red fire blazes, the grey smoke towers." I could almost smell leaves burning and see smoke drifting up into the sky. Some autumn poems are sad, but this one is happy. My favorite part is, "Sing a song of seasons! Something bright in all!" The message of this poem is that there is something special in each season all year long.

I felt cheerful when I read "Autumn Fires." It reminded me of fall days when my dad burns leaves in our backyard.

146 • Grade 2

Fog

The fog comes on
little cat feet.

It sits looking
over harbor and city
on silent haunches
and then moves on.

—*Carl Sandburg*

"Fog" is a poem by Carl Sandburg. It is a free verse poem, so it has no rhyme or pattern.

The poem is short and compares fog to a cat. My favorite part is the beginning. It says, "The fog comes on little cat feet." This means fog comes fast and quietly. It can appear and disappear very fast. The poem also compares fog to a cat sitting quietly.

I like the poem "Fog" because it made me feel quiet and sleepy, like I was wrapped in a soft, fuzzy blanket.

Note how the author of this piece:

- Wrote about the words in the poems and how the words made them feel.
  Some other ways to respond to a poem are:
  Tell how the poem reminds you of something that happened in your own life.
  Draw a picture to go with the poem.

Response to Poetry • 147

WRITING MODELS AND FORMS

Minilesson 133

Understanding the Response to Poetry

Common Core State Standard: W.2.1

Objective: Understand how to use the information given about the response to poetry.

Guiding Question: How can I use the information to help me write a strong response to poetry?

Teach/Model

Read aloud pp. 146–147. Add that a response to poetry may tell the writer's favorite part and explain why this part is special or important to the writer.

Practice/Apply

Read aloud the poem at the top of p. 146. Then work with children to find the author's opinions about the poem in the response.

Minilesson 134

Using Quotation Marks

Common Core State Standard: W.2.1

Objective: Use quotation marks around titles and exact words.

Guiding Question: How do I write the title of a poem and words that I copy from someone else's writing?

Teach/Model

Explain that sometimes a response to poetry may include a few exact words from the poem, which must be put in quotation marks. Also point out that the title of a poem has quotation marks around it.

Practice/Apply

Have children locate the titles and the exact words. Have them discuss placement of the quotation marks (before the first word and after the last).

Response to Literature

Response to Literature

When you write a **response to literature**, you write about a book you have read. One way to write a response is to compare yourself to a character in a book.

Parts of a Response to Literature

- An introduction that names the book and its author and tells what the book is about
- A body that explains how the writer and the character are alike and different
- A conclusion that tells how the writer feels about the character

Introduction
Tells what the book is about

Body
Tells how the writer and the character are alike and different

This paragraph tells how the writer and character are alike.

Alexander and Me

<u>Alexander and the Terrible, Horrible, No Good, Very Bad Day</u> is a book by Judith Viorst. It is about a boy named Alexander who has a bad day. He thinks that maybe it would be better if he moved to Australia. But his mom says that people in Australia have bad days, too.

Alexander and I are alike because we both have terrible, horrible, no good, very bad days. Some of the things that happened to Alexander have happened to me. For example, I had a cavity when I went to the dentist. I also got in trouble for fighting with my brothers. Alexander

This paragraph tells how the writer and character are different.

and I both hate lima beans, and we have pajamas that we don't like to wear.

Alexander and I are different in a few ways, too. My hair is black, and his is red. I don't chew gum, so I wouldn't get it stuck in my hair like Alexander did. My bad days have one or two bad things happen. Alexander had many bad things happen on his terrible, horrible, no good, very bad day. Also, I do not complain like Alexander. Finally, I wouldn't want to move to Australia. I think I would rather move to Texas.

Conclusion
Tells how the writer feels about the character

If Alexander were a real boy, I wouldn't mind being his friend. We could have fun skateboarding together. However, I think all of his complaining might get on my nerves sometimes.

Note how the author of this piece:

- Compared himself to Alexander. To **compare** means to tell how two things are alike.

- Gave examples:
  Some of the things that happened to Alexander have happened to me. For example. I had a cavity when I went to the dentist. I also got in trouble for fighting with my brothers.

WRITING MODELS AND FORMS

Minilesson 135

Introducing the Response to Literature

Common Core State Standard: W.2.1

Objective: Understand the characteristics of a good response to literature.

Guiding Question: What should I write to tell about a book?

Teach/Model

With children, read aloud pp. 148–149. Explain that examples from the book and examples from the writer's life are used to show ways in which the boys are alike and different.

Practice/Apply

Have children identify examples from the book and from the writer's life that show similarities and differences between the boys.

Minilesson 136

Organizing Similarities and Differences

Common Core State Standard: W.2.1

Objective: Use logical organization.

Guiding Question: What is the best way to organize my ideas in a response to literature?

Teach/Model

Tell children that one way to organize their ideas is to group similar ideas together. Point out that the student writer explained all of the ways he and the character are alike in one paragraph and all of the differences in another.

Practice/Apply

Have children locate the paragraph that contains similarities and the paragraph that contains differences.

Author Review

WRITING FORMS

Author Review

In an **author review**, the writer tells about books written by one author. The writer also tells his or her thoughts and feelings about the author's books.

Parts of an Author Review

- An introduction that gives the author's name
- A body that tells about the author's books and why the writer likes them
- A conclusion that sums up the writer's feelings about the author

Cynthia Rylant

Introduction
Names the author

Cynthia Rylant is my favorite author. My favorite books by Cynthia Rylant are the ones with Henry and Mudge. There must be a hundred Henry and Mudge books!

Her book Henry and Mudge: The First Book tells how Henry got Mudge. Henry didn't have brothers or sisters. There were no friends on his street. So, he asked his parents for a dog. They said yes! Henry got a puppy named Mudge. Mudge grew into a really big dog. When he licks Henry, it feels gooey and sticky. Cynthia Rylant put a sad part in this book when Mudge gets lost. But, she gave the book a happy ending

Body
Tells about the author's books and why the writer likes them

when Mudge is found. I like her happy endings.

In other Henry and Mudge books, Mudge is grown up. He and Henry have exciting adventures. In Henry and Mudge and the Sneaky Crackers, they are spies. In Henry and Mudge and the Tumbling Trip, they go on a trip to the Wild West. I like these stories because they make me use my imagination.

What I like best about Cynthia Rylant's books are the funny parts. Mudge is so big and playful that he makes messes wherever he goes. For example, in Henry and Mudge and the Bedtime Thumps, Mudge drools all over Grandma's dress, and he accidentally knocks a bowl of peppermints off the table.

Conclusion
Sums up the writer's feelings about the author

Cynthia Rylant's books are my favorites because I am an only child like Henry. I have a dog, and he is my best friend. I laugh when I read these books because Cynthia Rylant understands a boy and his dog.

WRITING MODELS AND FORMS

Minilesson 137

Understanding the Author Review

Common Core State Standard: W.2.1

Objective: Recognize the components of a good author review.

Guiding Question: How do I share my opinion about an author and his or her books?

Teach/Model

Read aloud and discuss pp. 150–151. Add that the author review tells readers what each of the stories is about and helps them understand the student writer's opinions and feelings about the author and her books.

Practice/Apply

Have children find examples from the model that explain the student writer's opinions and feelings about the author and her books.

Minilesson 138

Writing Book Titles

Common Core State Standard: W.2.1, L.2.2b

Objective: Understand conventions for writing book titles.

Guiding Question: How should I write the title of a book?

Teach/Model

Explain that the title of a book should be underlined. Point out the underlined title in the second paragraph. Add that when a title is typed on a computer, it is written in slanted letters called *italics.* Point out that all of the important words in a title are capitalized. Only small words such as *and* and *the* are not capitalized, unless they are the first words in the title.

Practice/Apply

Have children find the underlined titles in the model and review with them the rules about correct format.

Book Report/Poster That Persuades

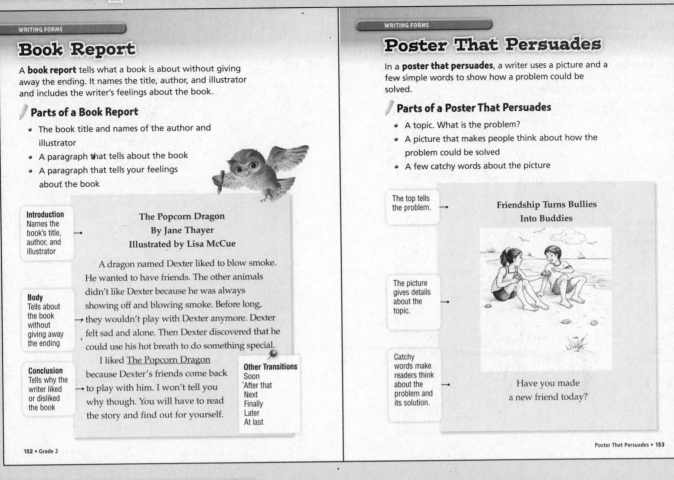

Book Report

A **book report** tells what a book is about without giving away the ending. It names the title, author, and illustrator and includes the writer's feelings about the book.

Parts of a Book Report
- The book title and names of the author and illustrator
- A paragraph that tells about the book
- A paragraph that tells your feelings about the book

Introduction Names the book's title, author, and illustrator

Body Tells about the book without giving away the ending

Conclusion Tells why the writer liked or disliked the book

The Popcorn Dragon
By Jane Thayer
Illustrated by Lisa McCue

A dragon named Dexter liked to blow smoke. He wanted to have friends. The other animals didn't like Dexter because he was always showing off and blowing smoke. Before long, they wouldn't play with Dexter anymore. Dexter felt sad and alone. Then Dexter discovered that he could use his hot breath to do something special.

I liked The Popcorn Dragon because Dexter's friends come back to play with him. I won't tell you why though. You will have to read the story and find out for yourself.

Other Transitions
Soon
After that
Next
Finally
Later
At last

152 • Grade 2

Poster That Persuades

In a **poster that persuades**, a writer uses a picture and a few simple words to show how a problem could be solved.

Parts of a Poster That Persuades
- A topic. What is the problem?
- A picture that makes people think about how the problem could be solved
- A few catchy words about the picture

The top tells the problem.

The picture gives details about the topic.

Catchy words make readers think about the problem and its solution.

Friendship Turns Bullies Into Buddies

Have you made a new friend today?

Poster That Persuades • 153

WRITING MODELS AND FORMS

Minilesson 139

Introducing the Book Report

Common Core State Standard: W.2.2

Objective: Understand how to write a book report.

Guiding Question: What information should I include when writing to tell about a book that I read?

Teach/Model

Read aloud p. 152. Explain that the details interest the audience without telling too much about what happens in the story. Point out the list of Other Transitions. Add that transitions help readers know the order that events happened in the book.

Practice/Apply

Have children identify the transitions in the student model (*Before long, Then*). Discuss which details make them want to read the book. (ex: *he could...do something special*).

Minilesson 140

Understanding the Persuasive Poster

Common Core State Standard: W.2.3

Objective: Use the page to understand a poster that persuades.

Guiding Question: What should I include on a persuasive poster?

Teach/Model

Read and discuss p. 153. Point out that the poster only includes a few words. Explain that the purpose is to allow the audience to understand the message quickly and easily and that the picture should help explain the writer's ideas.

Practice/Apply

Have children identify the problem and solution presented by the poster. Together, discuss how the picture supports these ideas.

Labels and Captions

Labels and Captions

A **label** names a picture. A **caption** tells more about a picture. A label uses just a few words. A caption includes one or more complete sentences.

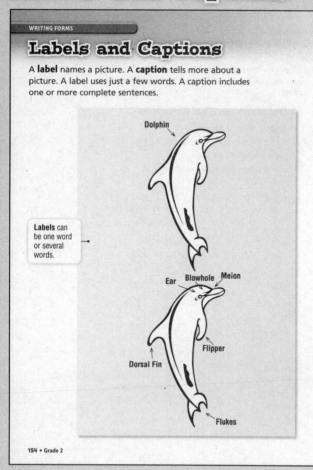

Dolphin

Labels can be one word or several words.

Ear   Blowhole   Meion

Flipper

Dorsal Fin

Flukes

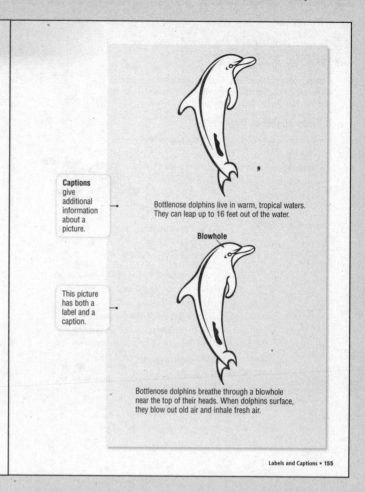

Captions give additional information about a picture.

Bottlenose dolphins live in warm, tropical waters. They can leap up to 16 feet out of the water.

Blowhole

This picture has both a label and a caption.

Bottlenose dolphins breathe through a blowhole near the top of their heads. When dolphins surface, they blow out old air and inhale fresh air.

WRITING MODELS AND FORMS

Minilesson 141

Understanding Labels and Captions

Common Core State Standard: W.2.2

Objective: Understand how to use labels and captions.

Guiding Question: How can I explain what a picture shows?

Teach/Model

Read and discuss pp. 154–155. Explain that these are examples of illustrations a writer might include in a report about dolphins. Pictures are often used to help an audience understand a writer's ideas. Point out the labels and captions. Explain that these tell information about what is shown in the pictures.

Practice/Apply

Have children discuss how the labels and captions are helpful in understanding the topic, dolphins.

Minilesson 142

Using Visual Aids

Common Core State Standard: W.2.2

Objective: Understand types of visual aids.

Guiding Question: What can I use to show my ideas?

Teach/Model

Explain that pp. 154–155 show examples of illustrations or pictures that a writer might use to help explain information about dolphins. Add that writers might also include graphs, maps, photos, charts, or tables to help the audience understand a topic.

Practice/Apply

Have children discuss how an illustration, graph, or map can help readers better understand information.

Notetaking Strategies

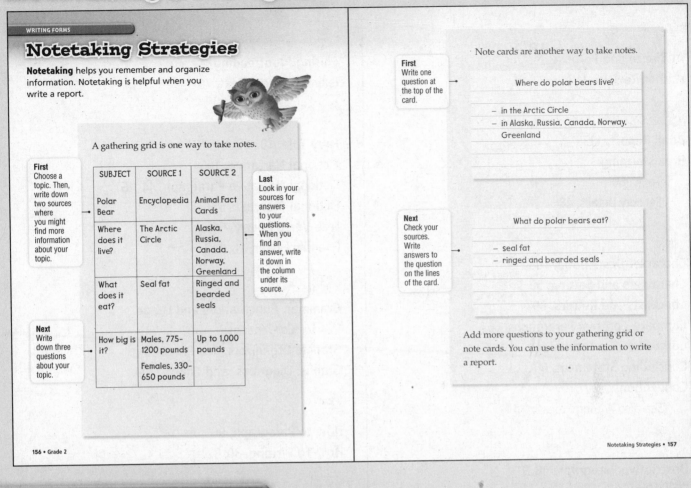

Notetaking Strategies

Notetaking helps you remember and organize information. Notetaking is helpful when you write a report.

A gathering grid is one way to take notes.

First
Choose a topic. Then, write down two sources where you might find more information about your topic.

SUBJECT	SOURCE 1	SOURCE 2
Polar Bear	Encyclopedia	Animal Fact Cards
Where does it live?	The Arctic Circle	Alaska, Russia, Canada, Norway, Greenland
What does it eat?	Seal fat	Ringed and bearded seals
How big is it?	Males, 775–1200 pounds Females, 330–650 pounds	Up to 1,000 pounds

Last
Look in your sources for answers to your questions. When you find an answer, write it down in the column under its source.

Next
Write down three questions about your topic.

Note cards are another way to take notes.

First
Write one question at the top of the card.

Where do polar bears live?
– in the Arctic Circle
– in Alaska, Russia, Canada, Norway, Greenland

Next
Check your sources. Write answers to the question on the lines of the card.

What do polar bears eat?
– seal fat
– ringed and bearded seals

Add more questions to your gathering grid or note cards. You can use the information to write a report.

156 • Grade 2

Notetaking Strategies • 157

WRITING MODELS AND FORMS

Minilesson 143

Understanding Notetaking Strategies

Common Core State Standards: W.2.7, W.2.8

Objective: Use the pages to recognize strategies for recording information.

Guiding Question: How can I record information?

Teach/Model

Read aloud pp. 156–157. Point out that questions are written in the first column of the chart, and the answers found in the sources are written beside each question. Add that when using note cards, children should write the sources where the information was found.

Practice/Apply

Have children discuss which strategy they would prefer to use to record information and why.

Minilesson 144

Selecting Sources for Research

Common Core State Standards: W.2.6, W.2.7, W.2.8

Objective: Recognize types of sources to use for research.

Guiding Question: Where can I find information about a topic?

Teach/Model

Explain that encyclopedias, newspapers, magazines, nonfiction books, textbooks, atlases, and the Internet are good sources for researching facts about a topic. Add that Internet sites ending with .org and .edu are usually trustworthy. Explain that different sources are good for finding different types of information.

Practice/Apply

Have children identify the sources used by the student writer. Discuss other possible sources for facts about polar bears.

Writing for Common Core • 115

Index